Strategic MICE Management

Strategic MICE Management

발 행 | 2024 년 1 월 3 일
저 자 | Nahyun Lee, PhD
펴낸이 | 한건희
펴낸곳 | 주식회사 부크크
출판사등록 | 2014.07.15.(제 2014-16 호)
주 소 | 서울특별시 금천구 가산디지털 1 로 119 SK 트윈타워 A 동 305 호
전 화 | 1670-8316
이메일 | info@bookk.co.kr

ISBN | 979-11-410-6392-4

www.bookk.co.kr

Strategic
MICE
Management

Nahyun Lee, PhD

CONTENTS

FOREWORD

"Welcome to the captivating world of Meetings, Incentives, Conferences, and Exhibitions—commonly known as MICE. This book is your passport to understanding the ins and outs of planning these special events, a realm where professionals in the hospitality industry excel. As you embark on this journey, this book will guide you step-by-step, unraveling the complexities and sharing valuable insights. Discover the nuances of different MICE events and master the art of planning with this comprehensive guide. By the end of this book, you will not only be well versed in MICE but also equipped to display your knowledge by planning your very own special event.

Special thanks go to my family, whose unwavering support and trust have been my pillars of strength throughout this journey. A heartfelt thank you to Jihun, whose presence and encouragement has been a constant source of inspiration. This book is a testament to the power of family and the belief that propels us forward. Thank you for being my rock and my motivation."

EVENT PLANNING SKILLS YOU NEED

Tick the boxes that highlight your unique abilities.

Organizational Skills

☐ Manages multiple tasks and details simultaneously.

☐ Proficient in creating and maintaining schedules, and budgets.

Communication Skills

☐ Possesses strong verbal and written communication skills.

☐ Can negotiate and liaise effectively with clients, and vendors.

Creativity

☐ Displays innovative thinking to develop unique and engaging event concepts.

☐ Exhibits problem-solving skills to address unexpected challenges during events.

Time Management

☐ Efficiently manages time to meet deadlines.

☐ Prioritizes tasks to focus on critical activities and delegates responsibilities effectively.

Customer Service Orientation

☐ Maintains a focus on providing customer service to clients.

☐ Anticipates and addresses client needs and concerns.

1. UNDERSTANDING MICE INDUSTRY

From Convening to Modern Gatherings

The term convention has its roots in the Latin word conventio, which is derived from the verb convenire. Conventio refers to a meeting or assembly, and convenire means to come together. Over time, these Latin roots evolved into the word convention in English and other languages.

The concept of conventions as formal meetings or gatherings dates back centuries and has been a part of various societies and cultures. The term has been applied to different types of gatherings, ranging from political assemblies and religious meetings to trade shows and conferences.

In the context of the hospitality and events industry, convention specifically refers to a large formal assembly or gathering of people with a common interest, purpose, or profession. Conventions can encompass various events, including meetings, seminars, conferences, and exhibitions. The term has become widely used to describe organized and planned gatherings that bring together individuals for networking, knowledge sharing, and collaboration.

The evolution of the term convention reflects the historical and linguistic development of the concept of people coming together for a shared purpose, and it has adapted to the diverse and dynamic nature of modern events and gatherings.

MICE vs. Convention Dynamics

MICE and Convention are related terms within the broader context of the hospitality and events industry, but they refer to different concepts. A convention typically refers to a formal meeting or assembly of individuals with a shared interest, purpose, or profession. Conventions can encompass various types of gatherings, including meetings, conferences, and exhibitions. The term convention is a general one and can be applied to a wide range of organized and planned gatherings where people come together for a specific purpose.

MICE is an acronym that specifically encompasses four different types of events—Meetings, Incentives, Conferences, and Exhibitions. It is a more comprehensive term that includes various forms of gatherings and events within the hospitality and events industry. MICE provides a framework to categorize and organize different types of events. Each component of MICE serves a specific purpose: meetings for discussion, incentives for motivation or reward, conferences for knowledge exchange, and exhibitions for showcasing products or services.

Key Differences are that Convention is a more general term

that can refer to any formal gathering, while MICE is a specialized term encompassing specific types of events. MICE breaks down the broader category of conventions into more specific components—meetings, incentives, conferences, and exhibitions. Convention emphasizes the idea of people coming together, while MICE goes further by categorizing events based on their distinct purposes.

In summary, convention is a broader term referring to formal gatherings, while MICE is a more specific framework that classifies events into distinct categories based on their purposes and characteristics.

MICE vs Convention	
MICE	Convention
Acronym: Meetings, Incentives, Conferences, and Exhibitions	Formal meeting or assembly
Comprehensive term for various forms of gatherings in hospitality	Encompasses meetings, conferences, exhibitions
Specialized term categorizing specific event types	General term for organized and planned gatherings
Framework categorizing Meetings, Incentives, Conferences, and Exhibitions	Broad application to a wide range of gatherings
Categorizes events based on their distinct purposes and characteristics	Emphasizes people coming together for a specific purpose

Standardization and Recognition

The term MICE is commonly used in Korea as well as in many other countries around the world. The MICE industry has gained widespread recognition as a comprehensive framework to categorize and manage various types of business events and gatherings. The MICE industry plays a significant role in the broader hospitality and tourism sectors. The countries host a variety of meetings, conferences, incentives, and exhibitions, attracting both domestic and international participants. The term MICE is widely understood and utilized in marketing, event planning, and tourism-related contexts to describe and promote these diverse business events.

Governments, industry associations, and event professionals in Korea actively promote and support the MICE industry as it contributes to economic development, business networking, and knowledge exchange. The use of the term reflects the global standardization of terminology within the events and hospitality sector.

While the term MICE is widely recognized and used in the events and hospitality industry, it is essential to acknowledge that its usage and popularity may vary across regions and countries. The extent to which MICE is commonly used can depend on local industry practices, terminology preferences, and cultural factors. In many countries, especially that with well-established event industries, MICE is a standard and widely understood term. However, in some regions or among certain professionals, alternative terms or variations may be preferred.

Interdisciplinary Synergies: Tourism and hospitality industry

The MICE industry is intricately connected to the tourism and hospitality sector, playing a pivotal role in shaping the overall landscape. MICE events serve as catalysts for destination attractiveness, drawing professionals, experts, and enthusiasts from various fields to a centralized location. As these events unfold, they generate substantial demand for hospitality services, including accommodations, dining, and transportation.

The infrastructure developed to accommodate large-scale conferences and exhibitions enhances a destination's appeal for both business and leisure travelers. Beyond the immediate economic impact during events, successful integration of the MICE industry contributes to long-term tourism trends, fostering sustained growth in local businesses and supporting the broader tourism ecosystem. The MICE industry, with its ability to attract diverse audiences and stimulate economic activities, stands as an integral component of the multifaceted tapestry that constitutes the tourism and hospitality industry.

The MICE industry serves as a dynamic bridge between leisure and business realms, embodying a multifaceted connection. On one hand, MICE events offer a structured platform for professionals to convene, share insights, and foster collaborations, thereby enhancing the efficacy of business activities. These gatherings act as catalysts for economic growth and global networking. On the other hand, the MICE industry significantly intersects with leisure, providing business travelers with opportunities for exploration and cultural engagement during their free time. The availability of recreational activities, cultural attractions, and entertainment options enhances the overall appeal of a destination, making it equally attractive for both business and leisure travelers. In essence, the MICE industry seamlessly integrates business and leisure dynamics, contributing to a comprehensive and enriching travel experience.

Leisure and tourism are the cornerstones of the travel industry, driving exploration and cultural exchange. When individuals embark on leisure trips, they often become tourists, contributing to the economic and cultural vitality of destinations. This overlap is particularly relevant in cities or regions hosting MICE events, as leisure opportunities abound for business travelers during their free time. The availability of recreational activities, cultural attractions, and entertainment options enhances the overall appeal of a destination for both business and leisure travelers.

Business travel acts as a catalyst for economic activities and global networking. Professionals attending conferences or corporate events contribute to the economic growth of host cities. The MICE industry, within the realm of business travel, plays a pivotal role in facilitating these interactions. It provides a structured platform for professionals to convene, share knowledge, and forge collaborations. The success of the MICE industry is intertwined with the effectiveness of business travel in fostering meaningful connections.

The MICE industry is a specialized subset of business travel with its own unique dynamics. MICE events attract professionals from various sectors, creating a convergence of expertise and ideas. Destinations hosting successful MICE events receive global recognition, attracting a blend of business and leisure travelers. The infrastructure developed for the MICE industry, including conference centers and exhibition halls, further enhances a destination's overall tourism appeal.

The synergy between leisure, tourism, business, and the MICE industry has profound economic implications. A thriving MICE industry stimulates economic growth in host cities by boosting hospitality, transportation, and local businesses. The economic impact extends beyond the duration of events, influencing long-term tourism trends. Effective destination management involves leveraging the interconnectedness of these factors to create a holistic and sustainable tourism ecosystem.

Decoding MICE Activities

Meetings are organized gatherings of individuals for the purpose of discussion, collaboration, decision-making, information sharing, or problem solving. Meetings can vary in scale and format, ranging from small team discussions to large corporate assemblies. There are five key characteristics of the meetings in the MICE context.

Purposeful Gathering: Meetings have a specific purpose, whether it is for sharing information, making decisions, brainstorming ideas, or fostering collaboration.

Interactivity: Attendees actively participate in discussions, contributing their insights, ideas, and feedback.

Structured Agenda: Meetings typically follow a structured agenda outlining topics to be discussed, ensuring a focused and organized discussion.

Varied Formats: Meetings can take on various formats, including team meetings, board meetings, committee meetings, and more, depending on the nature of the gathering.

Decision-Making: Some meetings involve decision-making processes where participants collectively make choices or come to agreements.

Within the realm of business gatherings, various types of meetings serve distinct purposes.

Board Meetings bring together a company's board of directors, fostering discussions on strategic decisions and matters related to corporate governance. These sessions are pivotal for shaping the direction and policies of the organization.

Team Meetings, on the other hand, are routine assemblies of work teams. These gatherings play a crucial role in coordinating activities, facilitating the exchange of updates, and addressing challenges collectively. Team meetings contribute to the overall cohesion and effectiveness of a work unit.

Committee Meetings involve specialized groups within an organization, such as project committees or task forces. These focused gatherings allow committee members to collaborate on specific projects, exchange expertise, and strategize solutions. Committee meetings are instrumental in driving targeted initiatives and achieving organizational objectives.

Incentive travels are a motivational tool that involves rewarding individuals, typically employees or students, for achieving specific goals or demonstrating exceptional performance. Rather than traditional forms of recognition, such as cash bonuses, incentive travel offers a unique and memorable experience as a way of acknowledging and celebrating accomplishments.

Incentive travel programs exhibit key characteristics that distinguish them within the realm of rewards and recognition. Primarily centered on a rewards-based approach, these programs offer participants the opportunity to indulge in travel experiences as a tangible acknowledgment of their accomplishments. A defining feature is the flexibility for customization, allowing program tailoring to align precisely with the preferences and interests of individual participants. This personalization ensures that the rewards are not only meaningful but resonate with the unique motivations of each individual.

The motivational impact of incentive travel is profound, as the prospect of an enriching travel experience serves as a potent catalyst, inspiring individuals to excel in their respective roles or tasks. Moreover, incentive travel programs can be structured to recognize either individual achievements or group accomplishments, offering versatility in catering to diverse goals and achievements within an organization.

Incentive travel encompasses diverse types tailored to recognize and motivate individuals or teams within various contexts. Recognition trips stand out as rewards for exceptional performance, surpassing sales targets, or reaching specific milestones. These trips often take participants to desirable destinations, providing a luxurious and memorable experience. Employee retreats, on the other hand, are designed to enhance team building and boost morale. These retreats blend work-related activities with leisure, creating a conducive environment for fostering stronger team dynamics. Additionally, education and training trips cater to academic contexts, with educational institutions utilizing incentive travel as part of study-abroad programs or rewards for academic excellence. Such trips offer students unique learning opportunities in different cultural and academic settings, adding an enriching dimension to their educational journey.

Conferences are formal gatherings that bring together professionals, experts, academics, and individuals with shared interests to discuss, exchange knowledge, and explore advancements within a specific industry, field of study, or area of interest. Conferences serve as platforms for learning, networking, and presenting research or innovations.

Conferences exhibit distinctive key characteristics that contribute to their significance in the realm of professional development. A fundamental aspect is the platform they offer for knowledge exchange, facilitating the sharing of insights, research findings, and expertise among participants. This collective learning environment enhances the overall depth of understanding within a field. Networking opportunities further enrich the conference experience, allowing attendees to connect with peers, industry leaders, and potential collaborators, thereby expanding their professional network.

The multidisciplinary nature of conferences is another key characteristic, as they often cover a broad spectrum of topics within a specific field, encouraging diverse discussions and collaborations. Participants contribute to these events through various presentation formats, including keynote speeches, paper presentations, workshops, and panel discussions, offering a dynamic and interactive exchange of ideas.

Within the landscape of conferences, different types cater to specific objectives and audiences. Academic conferences, for instance, focus on scholarly research and academic discussions, providing a platform for researchers and scholars to present their work and engage in intellectual discourse.

Industry conferences, on the other hand, target professionals within a specific industry, addressing trends, innovations, and best practices relevant to that sector. Lastly, International Conferences gather participants from around the world to delve into global issues, share diverse perspectives, and foster international collaboration, reflecting the expansive reach and impact of these events.

Exhibitions are structured events where businesses, organizations, and individuals display their products, services, or ideas to a targeted audience. Exhibitions provide a platform for direct interaction between exhibitors and attendees, facilitating product demonstrations, networking, and business promotion. Exhibitions encompass key characteristics that contribute to their role as dynamic platforms for industry interaction. A significant aspect is the product showcase, where exhibitors present their offerings, providing attendees with the opportunity to explore and interact with products or services firsthand.

This immersive experience enhances the understanding and appreciation of showcased items. Exhibitions also play a pivotal role in industry engagement by bringing together professionals, buyers, and sellers within a specific sector, fostering collaboration, and cultivating crucial business partnerships. Often used interchangeably with exhibitions, Trade Shows are a specific subset that concentrates on showcasing products and services within a particular industry or market, emphasizing the commercial aspect of these events. Networking opportunities further amplify the value of exhibitions, offering attendees the chance to connect with industry experts, potential clients, and suppliers, facilitating meaningful connections within the business landscape.

Various types of exhibitions cater to diverse objectives and audiences. Trade Exhibitions, for instance, are industry-specific events where companies present their products or services to potential buyers, distributors, and partners, driving business interactions. Art Exhibitions, on the other hand, focus on displaying visual arts, including paintings, sculptures, and other artistic expressions, providing a platform for artists to connect with the public. Consumer exhibitions, targeting the public, create direct engagement opportunities between businesses and consumers, fostering brand awareness and consumer relationships.

The Ripple Effect of MICE Industry Impact

The ripple effect, akin to expanding circles formed when a pebble is dropped into water, denotes the series of consequential impacts resulting from a single event or action. In the context of the MICE industry, the ripple effect represents the wide-ranging and interconnected outcomes that emanate from hosting impactful business events.

The MICE industry's ripple effect on the economy is profound. As business events attract a surge of participants, the demand for local services experiences a significant boost. Accommodation, transportation, catering, and entertainment sectors witness increased activity, leading to job creation and revenue generation for local businesses. Moreover, the development of infrastructure, such as convention centers and exhibition halls, required for hosting MICE events contributes to long-term economic growth, attracting investment and enhancing the overall economic landscape.

Internationally acclaimed MICE events hosted by a country amplify its political and diplomatic standing. The diplomatic ripple effect occurs as policymakers, industry leaders, and experts convene to discuss global issues, fostering collaboration and strengthening international relations. Successful organization of such events reflects positively on the host country's organizational prowess, influencing diplomatic perceptions and potentially opening avenues for increased cooperation with other nations.

The ripple effect of the MICE industry extends into the social fabric by providing a platform for knowledge exchange and cultural interaction. Conferences and seminars facilitate the dissemination of cutting-edge knowledge and advancements in various fields, contributing to intellectual and professional growth. The diverse participation in international MICE events introduces cultural diversity, fostering a more inclusive global community. Additionally, the social interactions within these events contribute to community development, as participants engage with local culture, support charitable activities, and leave lasting positive impressions.

The integrated impact of the MICE industry's ripple effect underscores its role as a catalyst for positive change. The economic, political/diplomatic, and social dimensions are not isolated but intricately interconnected. As economic growth stimulates infrastructure development, it enhances the appeal of a destination for future MICE events, creating a self-sustaining cycle of positive outcomes. This integrated impact positions the MICE industry as a dynamic force that extends beyond individual events, leaving a lasting imprint on the host community and the global stage.

The sustainability and potential of the MICE industry's ripple effect lie in its ability to foster enduring connections and contribute to the ongoing development of communities. As the positive outcomes accumulate over time, the MICE industry becomes a driving force for sustained economic growth, strengthened diplomatic ties, and enriched social fabric. Recognizing and maximizing this potential ensures that the ripple effect continues to shape the MICE landscape in ways that benefit local and global stakeholders alike.

Review Quiz

1. Convening Evolution

What is the origin of the term convention?

  a. Latin word convocare

  b. Latin word conventio

  c. Greek word symposium

  d. French word convenir

2. MICE vs. Convention

How does MICE differ from a traditional convention?

  a. MICE is an informal gathering, while conventions are formal.

  b. MICE is a specific type of convention, focusing on meetings.

  c. Conventions only involve conferences, while MICE includes various components.

  d. MICE and conventions are synonymous terms.

3. Standardization and Recognition

Why is standardization crucial for the MICE industry?

  a. To limit creativity and promote uniformity.

  b. To ensure events are identical globally.

  c. To enhance professionalism, quality, and global recognition.

  d. Standardization is not essential in the MICE industry.

4. Interdisciplinary Synergies

How does the MICE industry contribute to tourism and hospitality?

a. By limiting the influx of tourists.

b. By creating job opportunities only for event planners.

c. By attracting visitors, generating economic activity, and fostering growth.

d. MICE has no impact on tourism and hospitality.

5. Decoding MICE Activities

What does the I in MICE stand for?

a. Incentives

b. Industry

c. International

d. Integration

6. The Ripple Effect

What aspect of the MICE industry does the ripple effect primarily refer to?

a. The impact on local wildlife.

b. The interconnected outcomes stemming from hosting impactful business events.

c. The sound effects used in conferences.

d. The visual effects in exhibition displays.

Discussion Topic

Draw a mind map for MICE industry

A mind map is a visual representation that helps organize information and show the relationships between different concepts.

Tips!

The central theme is MICE Industry.

It branches out into four main components: Meetings, Incentives, Conferences, and Exhibitions. Each component further branches out into specific areas. For example, under Meetings, you have Corporate Meetings, and under Incentives, you have Event Planning Tools.

2. KEY STAKEHOLDERS OF THE MICE INDUSTRY

Professional Conference Organizers (PCOs)

Professional Conference Organizers (PCOs) serve as specialized entities dedicated to the comprehensive planning, organization, and execution of conferences and events. Their defining characteristics include a wealth of expertise in conference logistics and management, a commitment to customization according to client needs, and the ability to offer a wide range of services tailored to the unique requirements of each event. PCOs often operate on a global scale, enabling them to navigate diverse cultural landscapes and regulatory environments. The integration of technology is a hallmark of their approach, leveraging tools such as event apps and virtual platforms to enhance attendee experiences.

In their role, PCOs function as central coordinators, overseeing project management, logistics and operations, program development, financial management, marketing and promotion, and technology implementation. Efficient project management ensures a seamless execution of events, allowing clients to focus on their core responsibilities. With a commitment to professionalism, PCOs contribute to the enhancement of their clients' reputations, maximizing the impact of events and delivering cost-effective solutions. Their ultimate purpose lies in facilitating the success of conferences and events, introducing innovation to achieve goals, and ensuring a positive impact on attendees and stakeholders.

The extensive range of services provided by PCOs includes venue selection and management, program development, logistical operations, attendee management, financial planning, marketing and promotion, and post-event evaluation. This comprehensive approach makes PCOs a one-stop solution for organizations seeking professional and efficient event management services. As organizations increasingly recognize the importance of impactful events, the role of PCOs becomes pivotal in delivering high quality, successful conferences and ensuring a positive experience for all stakeholders involved.

Professional Conference Organizers (PCOs) undertake a multifaceted role in orchestrating successful conferences and events, encompassing a spectrum of duties and responsibilities. At the heart of their responsibilities is effective project management, where PCOs oversee the entire lifecycle of an event. This involves meticulous planning, establishing timelines, and ensuring the seamless execution of tasks from initial conceptualization to post-event evaluation. Their adept handling of event logistics includes venue selection and negotiation, transportation coordination, accommodation management, catering services, and on-site operations. PCOs ensure that every logistical element contributes to the smooth execution of the event.

In the realm of program development, PCOs collaborate closely with clients to craft a compelling event program. This involves the selection of keynote speakers, organization of sessions, creation of agendas, and alignment of content with the overarching goals and objectives of the event. Financial management is another key facet of their role, with PCOs entrusted to manage event budgets, negotiate costs, and optimize resource allocation. They work diligently to control expenses and ensure that the event stays within budget constraints while delivering a high-quality experience.

The active role of PCOs extends into marketing and promotion, where they contribute to the development of strategies and the creation of promotional materials. PCOs work towards establishing a strong event brand, attracting attendees, and securing sponsors to ensure a robust turnout. In the digital age, PCOs leverage technology to enhance various aspects of event management. They integrate event apps, virtual platforms, and online tools to streamline registration processes, facilitate communication, and provide attendees with a seamless and interactive experience.

PCOs take charge of efficient registration processes, managing attendee databases, and providing on-site registration services. This involves ensuring a smooth registration experience for participants and addressing their queries and needs. Following the conclusion of an event, PCOs conduct thorough post-event evaluations. This process includes assessing the overall success of the event, gathering feedback from participants and stakeholders, and identifying areas for improvement. The insights gained from these evaluations contribute to enhancing the planning and execution of future events.

The duties and responsibilities of PCOs are diverse, demanding a combination of organizational skills, industry expertise, and a keen eye for detail. As central coordinators, PCOs play an integral role in shaping positive event experiences and ensuring the success of conferences within the dynamic landscape of the MICE industry. Their commitment to excellence is reflected in their ability to meet and exceed the expectations of their clients and participants.

Professional Conference Organizers (PCOs)	
Definition	PCOs are specialized entities that plan, organize, and execute conferences and events.
Role	- Project management for conferences. - Logistical coordination for event operations. - Program development and speaker coordination. - Financial management and budgeting. - Marketing and promotion of conferences. - Technology integration for events. - Attendee and participant management.
Skills Required	- Event management expertise. - Project management skills. - Negotiation and contracting abilities. - Communication and interpersonal skills. - Financial planning and budgeting proficiency. - Marketing and promotional skills. - Technological proficiency for event apps and virtual platforms.

Professional Exhibition Organizers (PEOs)

Professional Exhibition Organizers (PEOs) are specialized entities dedicated to the comprehensive planning, coordination, and execution of exhibitions, trade shows, and expos. With a distinct expertise in managing large-scale events, PEOs serve as pivotal facilitators, bringing together businesses, industries, and professionals within a designated space to showcase products, services, and innovations.

PEOs are characterized by their adept understanding of the exhibition landscape, including market trends, industry dynamics, and participant expectations. Their agility and adaptability allow them to navigate the diverse needs of exhibitors and attendees, fostering an environment conducive to networking, business development, and knowledge exchange. PEOs often demonstrate a global reach, organizing exhibitions that attract participants from various regions and industries.

The role of PEOs extends beyond logistical coordination to encompass strategic planning and execution. As central coordinators, PEOs facilitate the entire exhibition process, from initial conceptualization to the post-event evaluation. They collaborate with exhibitors, sponsors, and venue providers to ensure a seamless and impactful event experience. PEOs actively contribute to shaping the layout and design of exhibition spaces, optimizing visibility and accessibility for exhibitors and attendees alike.

The primary purpose of PEOs is to create a dynamic platform that enables businesses and professionals to showcase their products, services, and innovations. By orchestrating exhibitions, PEOs aim to foster collaboration, business growth, and industry advancement. Exhibitions organized by PEOs serve as catalysts for knowledge sharing, market exploration, and the establishment of valuable connections within diverse sectors.

PEOs offer a comprehensive range of services tailored to the unique needs of exhibitors and the specific requirements of each exhibition. This includes strategic planning, venue selection, floor plan design, logistical coordination, marketing and promotion, attendee management, and post-event evaluation. PEOs excel in creating engaging and interactive exhibition spaces, utilizing technology, and implementing innovative solutions to enhance the overall visitor experience. They often leverage their industry expertise to curate specialized zones, thematic pavilions, and networking opportunities within the exhibition space.

Beyond the event itself, PEOs play a crucial role in facilitating pre and post-event communication, ensuring that exhibitors receive support in the lead-up to the exhibition and valuable insights afterward. Collaborating with stakeholders, including exhibitors, sponsors, and industry partners, PEOs contribute to the success and sustainability of exhibitions as powerful platforms for business growth and industry advancement.

In essence, Professional Exhibition Organizers (PEOs) are key drivers in the dynamic world of exhibitions, serving as architects of environments that foster innovation, collaboration, and business success. Their multifaceted role and purpose underscore their significance in shaping the landscape of industries through impactful and memorable exhibitions.

Professional Exhibition Organizers (PEOs) bear a myriad of duties and responsibilities, playing a central role in orchestrating successful exhibitions and trade shows. At the core of their responsibilities is the strategic planning and execution of events, from conceptualization to the post-event evaluation.

PEOs actively engage in strategic planning, collaborating with clients to define exhibition objectives, target audiences, and key performance indicators. They facilitate the entire event process, from selecting an appropriate venue to designing a floor plan that optimizes visibility for exhibitors and ensures a seamless flow for attendees. PEOs actively contribute to shaping the overall layout and design of exhibition spaces, considering factors like industry trends, participant flow, and thematic elements.

Logistical coordination is a critical aspect of the PEO's role. They manage the intricate details of venue logistics, including setup, booth allocation, and on-site operations. PEOs work closely with exhibitors and sponsors to ensure that their requirements are met, providing support in areas such as booth construction, utilities, and technical infrastructure.

Marketing and promotion are key components of PEO responsibilities. They develop and implement effective marketing strategies to attract exhibitors and attendees, create promotional materials, and establish a strong event brand. PEOs aim to maximize visibility for exhibitors, drawing in a diverse audience and facilitating meaningful connections within the industry.

Within the expansive range of services, PEOs excel in creating engaging and interactive exhibition spaces. Leveraging technology, they integrate innovative solutions to enhance the overall visitor experience. This includes implementing digital tools, interactive displays, and virtual components that elevate the exhibition's impact and relevance.

Beyond the event itself, PEOs facilitate pre and post-event communication. They support exhibitors in the lead-up to the exhibition, providing guidance, logistical assistance, and ensuring that their participation aligns with their goals. Post-event, PEOs conduct thorough evaluations, assessing the success of the exhibition, gathering feedback from participants, and identifying areas for improvement.

Collaborating with stakeholders, including exhibitors, sponsors, and industry partners, PEOs contribute to the success and sustainability of exhibitions as powerful platforms for business growth and industry advancement. In essence, the duties and responsibilities of PEOs are diverse, demanding a combination of organizational skills, industry expertise, and a keen understanding of the evolving landscape of exhibitions. As architects of dynamic environments, PEOs play an integral role in shaping positive experiences and ensuring the success of exhibitions within the dynamic MICE industry.

Professional Exhibition Organizers (PEOs)	
Definition	PEOs are specialized entities focused on the planning, coordination, and execution of exhibitions and trade shows.
Role	- Strategic planning for exhibitions. - Venue selection and floor plan design. - Logistical coordination for exhibition setup and operations. - Marketing and promotion of exhibitions. - Technology integration for interactive exhibition spaces. - Pre and post-event communication with exhibitors.
Skills Required	- Strategic planning and organizational skills. - Venue management and logistics expertise. - Marketing and promotional skills. - Creativity in exhibition space design. - Technology integration for interactive exhibitions. - Effective communication with exhibitors and stakeholders. - Post-event evaluation and feedback analysis.

Venues and Facilities

Venues and facilities are integral components of the events industry, providing the physical infrastructure and spaces where various gatherings, conferences, exhibitions, and social functions take place.

Venues refer to physical locations or spaces designed and equipped to host events, ranging from small meetings to large-scale conferences or exhibitions. Facilities encompass the amenities and services provided within these spaces, contributing to the overall event experience.

Venues vary widely in size, layout, and capabilities. Characteristics include flexible seating arrangements, technological infrastructure, accessibility, and adaptability to accommodate diverse event requirements. Facilities within venues may include audiovisual equipment, catering services, breakout rooms, and other amenities tailored to event needs.

The role of venues is to serve as the backdrop for events, providing a suitable and functional environment for gatherings. Venues play a central role in shaping the overall atmosphere, logistics, and success of an event. Facilities within venues complement this role by offering essential services and resources.

The primary purpose of venues is to create spaces conducive

to the objectives of the events they host. Whether facilitating knowledge exchange, fostering networking, or showcasing products, venues contribute to achieving the goals set by event organizers. The purpose of facilities is to enhance the convenience and experience of event participants, ensuring seamless operations and optimal engagement.

Venues offer a diverse range of services to meet the needs of event organizers. This includes venue rental, technical support, catering, and event planning assistance. Facilities encompass services such as audiovisual equipment, Wi-Fi connectivity, on-site staff support, and customizable seating arrangements.

Venues are responsible for providing a safe, functional, and appealing space for events. This involves coordinating logistics, ensuring proper setup, and adhering to safety regulations. Facilities within venues have the duty to maintain and operate amenities efficiently, addressing the needs of event organizers and participants.

Examples of venues include convention centers, hotels, conference halls, and dedicated event spaces. Convention centers, such as COEX Convention & Exhibition Center, BEXCO (Busan Exhibition and Convention Center), are designed to host large conferences and exhibitions. Hotels, like the Marriott or Seoul Dragon City often have meeting and ballroom spaces suitable for various events. Conference halls, like the Lotte World Tower in Seoul, are iconic venues known for hosting diverse events. Dedicated event spaces, such as the Dongdaemun Design Plaza (DDP) in Seoul, cater to specific event requirements.

In summary, venues and facilities are pivotal components in the events industry, providing the canvas upon which diverse gatherings come to life. Their roles, characteristics, and services contribute significantly to the success of events, making them essential partners for event organizers and participants alike.

Service Providers

Service providers are crucial entities in the events industry, offering a diverse range of services that contribute to the planning, execution, and success of various events. These providers play a vital role in ensuring that events meet the expectations of organizers and participants alike.

Service providers encompass a broad category of businesses and professionals that offer specialized services to support the diverse needs of events. These services can range from event planning and logistics to technology, catering, and entertainment.

Service providers are characterized by their expertise in specific areas of event management. They are often highly specialized, bringing a depth of knowledge and skills to their respective fields. Flexibility, adaptability, and a customer-centric approach are key characteristics, as service providers tailor their offerings to meet the unique requirements of each event.

The role of service providers is to act as partners in the event planning process, collaborating with organizers to deliver seamless and memorable experiences. They contribute specialized knowledge and resources, enhancing the overall quality of events. Service providers can be involved in various stages of event execution, from pre-planning to on-site support.

The primary purpose of service providers is to fill specific roles within the event ecosystem, addressing key needs such as logistics, technology, catering, entertainment, and more. Their contributions aim to elevate the overall event experience, ensuring that organizers can rely on expert support to execute successful and impactful events.

Service providers offer a vast array of services to cater to different aspects of event management. These services may include event planning and coordination, audiovisual and technical support, catering, venue management, transportation logistics, security services, marketing and promotion, and entertainment.

The duties and responsibilities of service providers vary based on their areas of specialization. Event planning and coordination service providers may be responsible for creating comprehensive event plans, timelines, and coordinating logistics. Technical support providers ensure the seamless integration of audiovisual equipment and technology. Catering services handle menu planning, food preparation, and service during events. Security services are responsible for maintaining a safe environment, and marketing providers contribute to promotional efforts.

In essence, service providers form an indispensable part of the events industry, contributing their expertise to ensure the seamless execution of events and the satisfaction of all stakeholders involved. Their diverse roles and services collectively contribute to the success and impact of events across various sectors and scales.

Sponsors and Exhibitors

Sponsors and exhibitors play pivotal roles in the success of events, contributing significantly to the financial and experiential aspects of various gatherings, conferences, and exhibitions.

Sponsors are organizations or entities that provide financial support, goods, or services to an event in exchange for visibility and promotional opportunities. Exhibitors, on the other hand, are entities that showcase their products, services, or innovations in designated spaces within an event, interacting directly with attendees.

Sponsors are characterized by their willingness to invest in events to gain exposure, brand visibility, and positive association with the event's objectives. Exhibitors are distinguished by their desire to present and promote their offerings directly to a targeted audience within the event space.

The role of sponsors is multifaceted, encompassing financial support, brand promotion, and often, active participation in event activities. Sponsors contribute to the overall success of events by providing resources that enable organizers to enhance the quality and scale of the event. Exhibitors play a critical role in engaging with attendees, showcasing products or services, and fostering business connections.

The purpose of sponsors is to align their brand with the event's goals, increase visibility, and reach a targeted audience. Sponsors often seek to enhance brand image and generate positive associations by supporting events that align with their values or target demographic. Exhibitors aim to achieve various objectives, including product promotion, lead generation, market research, and networking opportunities.

Sponsors typically offer financial contributions, in-kind services, or resources that directly contribute to the event's success. This may include sponsoring specific sessions, providing branded materials, or supporting promotional activities. Exhibitors offer products, services, or innovations within designated booths or spaces, often accompanied by marketing collateral, demonstrations, and interactive experiences.

Sponsors have the responsibility to fulfill their financial commitments, actively engage with event organizers to optimize their visibility, and adhere to any contractual obligations. Exhibitors are responsible for creating engaging displays, providing accurate and attractive information about their offerings, and ensuring a positive and interactive experience for event attendees.

Examples of sponsors in South Korea include major corporations like Samsung, Hyundai, and LG, which frequently sponsor various events and conferences in the country. These companies contribute financially and often showcase their latest technologies or innovations. In the realm of exhibitions, companies like KOTRA (Korea Trade-Investment Promotion Agency) actively participate as exhibitors in trade shows, promoting Korean businesses and products on an international scale. Global brands like Amorepacific, a leading beauty and cosmetics company, frequently act as both sponsors and exhibitors, supporting events while showcasing their products.

In conclusion, sponsors and exhibitors are integral to the vibrancy of the events industry, playing key roles in supporting, enhancing, and showcasing the diverse offerings of the country's businesses and industries. Their collaborative efforts contribute to the success and impact of events on both a national and global scale.

Government and Regulatory Bodies

Within the realm of Meetings, Incentives, Conferences, and Exhibitions (MICE), government and regulatory bodies emerge as pivotal stakeholders entrusted with shaping and supporting the industry's regulatory landscape. These entities, operating at various levels, play a crucial role in fostering a conducive environment for MICE activities while ensuring compliance with laws, standards, and regulations.

In the context of the MICE industry, government and regulatory bodies take on the responsibility of formulating and supporting policies that facilitate the seamless execution of international conferences, events, and exhibitions. They contribute to the industry's governance by creating frameworks that promote fairness, transparency, and accountability.

The distinct characteristics of these bodies within the MICE sector include their authority to establish rules and standards, enforce compliance, and a commitment to safeguarding the public interest. Possessing legal and investigative capabilities, they actively monitor and regulate activities to uphold industry standards and ethical practices.

Government and regulatory bodies actively engage in policy development to support Professional Conference Organizers (PCOs), offering guidance on best practices, licensing procedures, and adherence to industry standards. Their multifaceted role involves overseeing licensing, conducting inspections, and addressing issues related to public health, safety, and the environment specific to MICE events.

The primary purpose remains aligned with fostering a regulatory environment that instills public trust, ensures economic stability, and promotes social well-being within the MICE industry. Their services span policy development, legislative oversight, licensing, inspection, enforcement, and dispute resolution, all geared towards maintaining the industry's integrity.

In fulfilling their duties, these bodies collaborate closely with MICE stakeholders, including PCOs, venues, and event planners. They seek input, address concerns, and adapt regulations to evolving circumstances, striking a delicate balance between supporting economic growth and safeguarding the unique interests of the MICE industry.

In essence, government and regulatory bodies emerge as key stakeholders actively influencing the regulatory landscape of the MICE industry. Through policy formulation, enforcement, and collaboration, they contribute to the industry's stability, ethical conduct, and overall prosperity, ensuring a favorable environment for sustainable development and societal well-being.

Beyond their regulatory roles, government and regulatory bodies in the MICE industry actively engage in advocacy and collaboration. They serve as proponents for the industry's growth, working closely with Professional Conference Organizers (PCOs), venues, and stakeholders to amplify its impact. By advocating for policies that encourage international conferences and events, they contribute to the industry's global prominence.

Destination Management Organizations (DMOs)

Destination Management Organizations (DMOs) are entities dedicated to the strategic development, promotion, and management of a specific destination, typically a city, region, or country. DMOs play a crucial role in shaping the visitor experience, fostering economic growth, and ensuring the sustainable development of tourism within a destination.

A Destination Management Organization (DMO) is a public or private organization responsible for coordinating and overseeing the planning, marketing, and management of a destination to attract visitors and enhance the overall visitor experience.

Key characteristics of DMOs include their focus on destination-level planning, collaboration with stakeholders, a customer-centric approach, and a commitment to sustainable tourism practices. DMOs often operate as non-profit organizations or public-private partnerships.

The role of DMOs is multifaceted. They act as strategic leaders, working to align the interests of various stakeholders, including businesses, local communities, and governments, to create a cohesive and appealing destination. DMOs also serve as destination marketers, promoting the destination to target audiences and attracting visitors through effective branding and marketing strategies.

The primary purpose of DMOs is to enhance the competitiveness and attractiveness of a destination. They aim to drive economic growth by increasing tourism-related revenues, creating jobs, and stimulating investment. DMOs also strive to balance the economic benefits of tourism with the preservation of cultural and natural resources, promoting responsible and sustainable tourism practices.

DMOs offer a diverse range of services to achieve their goals. This includes destination marketing and promotion, visitor services, event planning and support, research and data analysis, partnership development, and stakeholder engagement. DMOs may also be involved in infrastructure development, policy advocacy, and the creation of tourism-related experiences and products.

The duties and responsibilities of DMOs encompass various aspects of destination management. They are responsible for creating and implementing destination-marketing strategies, collaborating with businesses to develop tourism products and experiences, providing visitor information and support services, and conducting research to inform decision-making.

DMOs often play a pivotal role in coordinating and hosting events, festivals, and conferences that contribute to the destination's appeal. Additionally, they advocate for policies that support sustainable tourism development, foster community engagement, and ensure the long-term success of the destination.

In summary, Destination Management Organizations play a central role in shaping the tourism landscape of a destination. Through strategic planning, marketing, and collaboration, DMOs contribute to the economic vitality, cultural preservation, and overall sustainability of the destinations they represent. Their efforts are instrumental in creating memorable and positive experiences for visitors while balancing the interests of local communities and businesses.

Convention and Visitors Bureaus (CVBs)

Convention and Visitors Bureaus (CVBs) are organizations dedicated to promoting a specific destination to attract visitors, meetings, conventions, and events. Also known as Destination Marketing Organizations (DMOs), CVBs play a key role in driving tourism and business-related activities to a particular area.

A Convention and Visitors Bureau (CVB) is a destination marketing organization responsible for promoting and marketing a specific location to attract tourists, business travelers, and event planners. CVBs serve as the primary point of contact for those seeking information and support related to visiting or hosting events in a destination.

CVBs typically operate as non-profit organizations or public-private partnerships. They possess in-depth knowledge of their destination, maintain strong relationships with local stakeholders, and leverage marketing strategies to enhance the destination's appeal. CVBs are often customer-focused, aiming to provide comprehensive support and services to visitors and event planners.

The role of a CVB is multifaceted. CVBs act as destination marketers, promoting the unique attributes and offerings of their location to a wide audience. They serve as intermediaries between visitors, event planners, and local businesses, facilitating the planning and execution of various activities, including conventions, conferences, and leisure travel.

The primary purpose of CVBs is to boost the economic impact of tourism and events in their destination. By attracting visitors, conferences, and conventions, CVBs contribute to increased spending on local accommodations, dining, entertainment, and other services. CVBs also aim to enhance the destination's reputation, drive job creation, and support overall economic development.

CVBs offer a comprehensive range of services to meet the needs of visitors and event planners. These services include destination marketing and promotion, assistance with event planning and logistics, providing visitor information, coordinating site visits, facilitating partnerships with local businesses, and supporting the development of tourism-related products and experiences.

The duties and responsibilities of CVBs encompass various

aspects of destination marketing and management. CVBs conduct market research to identify target audiences and trends, develop marketing campaigns to promote the destination, and collaborate with local businesses and organizations to enhance the visitor experience. They also assist event planners with logistics, securing venues, coordinating accommodations, and promoting the destination as a suitable host for conferences and conventions.

CVBs actively engage with stakeholders, including government entities, local businesses, and community organizations, to align strategies and foster collaboration. They may also advocate for policies that support the growth of tourism and events while ensuring the sustainability and well-being of the destination.

In summary, Convention and Visitors Bureaus play a vital role in driving tourism and business activities to a destination. Through strategic marketing, collaboration, and comprehensive services, CVBs contribute to the economic vitality, reputation, and overall appeal of the locations they represent. Their efforts create positive experiences for visitors while supporting the growth and development of local communities.

Regional MICE Alliance in Korea		
No.	Region	URL
1	Seoul	korean.miceseoul.com
2	Busan	www.bto.or.kr/cvb
3	Daegu	www.daegucvb.com
4	Incheon	cvb.visitincheon.or.kr
5	Gwangju	www.gjto.or.kr
6	Daejeon	www.djto.kr
7	Ulsan	www.uto.or.kr
8	Gyeonggi	www.gmice.or.kr
9	Gangwon	www.gwto.or.kr
10	Jeonnam	www.ijnto.or.kr
11	Gyeongnam	www.gnto.or.kr
12	Jeju	www.jejucvb.or.kr
13	Goyang	www.goyangcvb.com
14	Suwon	www.scc.or.kr
15	Gyeongju	www.crowncity.kr
16	Gangneung	www.gtdc.or.kr
17	Jeonbuk	www.jbmice.or.kr

Source: https://koreaconvention.org:8090/eng/engmain.kc

Review Quiz

1. Professional Conference Organizers (PCOs)

What is the primary role of a PCO?

a. Marketing and promotion

b. Event planning and execution

c. Venue management

d. Sponsorship acquisition

2. Convention and Visitors Bureaus (CVBs)

What is the main purpose of a CVB?

a. Facilitating government regulations

b. Promoting and marketing a destination

c. Providing event planning services

d. Offering legal advice to event organizers

3. Service Providers

What is a key characteristic of service providers in the events industry?

a. Narrow specialization

b. Limited adaptability

c. No focus on customer satisfaction

d. Minimal collaboration with event organizers

4. Sponsors and Exhibitors

What is the primary purpose of sponsors in the events industry?

a. Providing event planning services

b. Attracting attendees to events

c. Gaining visibility and promoting brands

d. Offering catering services

5. Venues and Facilities

What is a characteristic of venues and facilities in the events industry?

a. Limited technological capabilities

b. Lack of diversity in event spaces

c. Versatility in hosting different types of events

d. Low capacity for accommodating attendees

6. Destination Management Organizations (DMOs)

What is the role of a Destination Management Organization (DMO) in the tourism industry?

a. Providing legal advice to tourists

b. Overseeing government regulations

c. Promoting and managing a destination

d. Offering transportation services

Discussion Topic

Analyzing an Exhibition

Guidelines for Group Discussion:

1. Choose an Exhibition

Pick a recent or upcoming exhibition with enough information on its official website.

2. Basic Exhibition Details

Share the basics:

ex. When and where did it happen or will happen?

ex. How long did it last or will last?

ex. How many people participated?

3. Why Attend or Exhibit?

Discuss why exhibitors or attendees would want to be part of this exhibition.

ex. Look for clues on the website about networking opportunities, potential business growth etc.

4. Business Model Insights

Look into how the exhibition makes money.

ex. Check for registration fees for exhibitors and attendees, sponsorship details, any other revenue strategies, etc.

5. Side Events and Entertaining factors etc.

3. MICE MASTERY: SIX STEPS TO EVENT SUCCESS

RESEARCH: At a glance

☐ Purpose

Understanding Event Context

Identifying Objectives and Expectations

☐ Activities

Market Research/ Stakeholder Surveys/ Competitor Analysis

☐ Outcome

Comprehensive Understanding

Clear Objectives

Risk Assessment

☐ Challenges and Considerations

Changing Trends/ Bias in Surveys/ Data Security

☐ Tips for Success

Engage Diverse Perspectives

Utilize Technology

Iterative Process

☐ Key Questions to Answer

- Who is the target audience, and what are their preferences?

- What are the goals and objectives of the event?

- Are there any potential challenges or risks that need to be
  addressed?

In the initial stage of MICE management, research serves as the foundational pillar, guiding the subsequent phases of event planning and execution. The primary purpose of research is to gain a comprehensive understanding of the event's context, requirements, and the expectations of its target audience. By delving into this phase with a strategic mindset, event organizers can align their efforts with the unique needs of the participants and stakeholders.

Activities in the research phase involve a multifaceted approach. Market research plays a pivotal role, allowing organizers to analyze industry trends, emerging preferences, and potential challenges that may influence the success of the event. Surveys and interviews with prospective attendees provide valuable insights into their preferences, expectations, and the factors influencing their decision to participate. Additionally, thorough examination of competitor events aids in benchmarking, helping organizers identifies opportunities for differentiation and improvement.

The outcome of the research phase is a nuanced understanding of the landscape in which the event will unfold. This encompasses a detailed profile of the target audience, insights into prevailing industry trends, and a comprehensive view of potential challenges and opportunities. Armed with this knowledge, event organizers can make informed decisions in the subsequent stages of MICE management, ensuring that the event is not only relevant but also resonant with the expectations of its audience.

Moreover, the research phase lays the groundwork for strategic decision-making, influencing critical elements such as event concept, design, and planning. Through a meticulous exploration of the event's ecosystem, organizers can tailor their approach to align with the preferences and expectations of the participants, creating a solid foundation for a successful MICE event.

In summary, the research phase is a critical starting point in MICE management, providing organizers with the insights needed to shape a compelling event experience. The purposeful integration of market research, participant feedback, and competitor analysis equips event planners with a robust understanding of the environment, fostering informed decision-making that resonates with the target audience and ensures the event's success.

Why Research

The research stage is essential because it sets the stage for informed decision-making, risk mitigation, and the development of a strategic and well-targeted event. It ensures that the subsequent stages of MICE management are built on a solid foundation, increasing the likelihood of a successful and impactful event.

Understanding Event Context

Research provides a comprehensive understanding of the context in which the event will take place. This includes the industry landscape, market trends, and the broader environment. Without this understanding, event organizers may miss opportunities or face unexpected challenges.

Clarifying Objectives and Expectations

Research helps in defining and clarifying the goals and objectives of the event. It allows the organizing team to articulate what they aim to achieve and sets the foundation for the entire event planning process.

Identifying Target Audience

By conducting research, event organizers can identify and understand their target audience. This includes demographics, preferences, and expectations. Knowing the audience is essential for tailoring the event to meet their needs and interests.

Risk Assessment

Research enables the identification of potential risks and challenges that may arise during the event. By anticipating these challenges, organizers can develop proactive strategies to mitigate risks and ensure the smooth execution of the event.

Informed Decision-Making

The insights gained from research inform decision-making at every stage of event planning. From choosing the right venue to designing the event program, data-driven decisions based on thorough research contribute to the overall success of the event.

Benchmarking Against Competitors

Research involves analyzing competitor events to understand what has worked well for them and where they may have faced challenges. This benchmarking helps organizers position their event strategically and incorporate successful elements from similar events.

Optimizing Resource Allocation

With a clear understanding of the market and audience, organizers can optimize the allocation of resources, both in terms of budget and personnel. This ensures that resources are directed toward activities and elements that will have the most significant impact on the event's success.

Adaptability to Trends

The events industry is dynamic, and trends can change rapidly. Research allows organizers to stay informed about current trends, enabling them to adapt their event plans to align with the latest industry developments and attendee expectations.

Building Stakeholder Confidence

Stakeholders, including sponsors, participants, and partners, often seek assurance that the event is well-planned and aligned with their interests. Research provides a solid foundation and instills confidence in stakeholders that the event is based on a thorough understanding of the market.

Research Approach

Conducting effective research for MICE management involves a systematic and thorough approach. Here are some key steps and considerations for the research process.

Define Research Objectives

Clearly outline the objectives of your research. What specific information are you seeking? Whether it's understanding market trends, identifying target audiences, or assessing competitor events, having clear objectives will guide your research efforts.

Utilize Secondary Research

Start by gathering existing information through secondary

research. This includes industry reports, academic papers, and articles related to MICE events. Online databases, industry associations, and government publications can be valuable sources.

Conduct Stakeholder Surveys

Develop surveys to gather insights from key stakeholders, including potential attendees, sponsors, and partners. Use a mix of open-ended and close-ended questions to capture both qualitative and quantitative data.

Analyze Competitor Events

Study competitor events to understand their strengths and weaknesses. Analyze their event programs, marketing strategies, and participant feedback. This can provide valuable benchmarks for your own event.

Engage in Focus Groups

Organize focus group discussions with representatives from your target audience. These discussions can provide in-depth qualitative insights into preferences, expectations, and potential pain points.

Social Media Listening

Monitor social media platforms for discussions related to your industry and event type. Social media listening tools can help you track trends, sentiment, and popular topics among your target audience.

Collaborate with Industry Experts

Reach out to industry experts, consultants, or professionals with experience in MICE management. Their insights and expertise can offer valuable perspectives on industry trends and best practices.

Attend Industry Events and Conferences

Participate in relevant industry events and conferences to network with professionals, observe event dynamics, and stay updated on the latest trends. These events provide firsthand experiences and insights.

Explore Online Forums and Communities

Engage with online forums, discussion groups, and communities related to event planning. These platforms can provide insights into challenges faced by organizers and solutions adopted in the industry.

Collate and Analyze Data

Systematically organize and analyze the gathered data. Use tools such as spreadsheets or dedicated research software to manage and analyze both qualitative and quantitative data.

Iterative Process

Treat the research process as iterative. As you gather information, be open to refining your research objectives and approach based on emerging insights. This adaptability enhances the quality of your research.

Ensure Ethical Considerations

Respect privacy and ethical considerations in your research. If collecting personal data, ensure compliance with data protection regulations and obtain informed consent from participants.

By following these steps, you can conduct thorough and effective research for MICE management, ensuring that the insights gathered inform strategic decision-making throughout the event planning process.

DESIGN: At a glance

☐ Purpose

Creating a distinctive and memorable event identity

Structuring the functional and experiential aspects

☐ Activities

Theme Development/ Visual Identity Creation

Event Program and Agenda Design/Event Space Planning

☐ Outcome

Comprehensive and integrated vision

A detailed event program/ Event space

☐ Challenges and Considerations

Balancing creativity with practicality

Staying within budget constraints/

Design elements for event's purpose

☐ Tips for Success

Effective collaboration and communication/ Regular meetings

Staying abreast of design trends and technologies

☐ Key Questions to Answer

- What visual elements will form the core of the event's brand identity?

- In what ways can the physical event space enhance the overall experience?

The design process in MICE management plays a pivotal role in shaping the overall experience and success of the event. At its core, the purpose of the design stage is twofold: to create a visual and thematic identity for the event and to outline the structural and logistical aspects that guide the event's flow and engagement strategies.

The first step in the design process involves developing a compelling event theme, serving as the narrative thread that ties together all elements. This theme encapsulates the essence of the occasion and provides a unifying concept for the subsequent design activities. Designers then collaborate to create a cohesive visual identity for the event, encompassing logos, branding materials, and promotional content. This visual identity not only captures attention but also communicates the event's purpose and values.

Moving beyond aesthetics, the design process encompasses the development of the event program and agenda. Working closely with content creators and subject matter experts, designers structure the sequence of activities, schedule speakers, panel discussions, and incorporate networking opportunities. Simultaneously, designers focus on planning the physical event space, ensuring it complements the chosen theme and facilitates intended interactions. Considerations include decor, lighting, seating arrangements, and interactive elements that enhance participant engagement.

The outcome of the design process is a comprehensive and integrated vision for the event. Visually, this includes a distinctive brand identity that captures attention and communicates the event's purpose. Logistically, the outcome is a detailed event program that ensures a smooth and engaging experience for attendees. The event space, designed in line with the chosen theme, becomes a dynamic and immersive environment that enhances participant experience. Collateral developed during this stage reinforces the brand identity and provides essential information about the event.

Designing an event involves challenges such as balancing creativity with practicality, staying within budget constraints, and ensuring that design elements enhance rather than distract from the event's purpose. Effective collaboration between designers, planners, and content creators is crucial to harmonize visual and experiential aspects. Success in event design often hinges on effective communication and staying abreast of design trends and technologies to infuse fresh and innovative elements into the event experience. Ultimately, the design process is about creating an immersive and cohesive event that captivates attendees, aligns with objectives, and leaves a lasting impression.

Why Design

The design stage is important in MICE management because it goes beyond aesthetics; it serves as a strategic and experiential foundation for the entire event. By carefully crafting the visual identity and structuring the event's elements, the design stage contributes significantly to the success, impact, and long-term recognition of the event.

Establishing Event Identity

The design stage is instrumental in creating a unique and recognizable identity for the event. Through the development of a compelling theme, visual elements, and branding materials, it sets the tone and personality of the event. This identity helps the event stand out in a crowded landscape and facilitates easy recognition among the target audience.

Aligning with Objectives

Event design ensures that all visual and experiential elements align with the overall objectives of the event. It serves as a strategic framework that guides the planning and execution of the event, ensuring that every aspect contributes to the intended goals and outcomes.

Enhancing Participant Engagement

A well-designed event has the power to captivate and engage participants. By carefully planning the event program, agenda, and physical space, the design stage creates an environment that encourages interaction, networking, and a positive overall experience. Engaged participants are more likely to derive value from the event and contribute to its success.

Communicating Purpose and Values

Design elements, including logos, branding materials, and event collateral, serve as visual cues that communicate the purpose and values of the event. Effective design ensures that attendees grasp the core messages and themes, fostering a deeper connection with the event's mission.

Differentiating from Competitors

In a competitive events landscape, a well-executed design sets an event apart from competitors. It helps create a memorable and distinctive experience, making a lasting impression on attendees. A strong visual identity can also contribute to the event's long-term brand recognition.

Facilitating Logistics and Operations

Design is not limited to aesthetics; it also involves the practical organization of the event. The layout of the event space, seating arrangements, and other logistical considerations are part of the design process. This ensures that the physical aspects of the event support the flow of activities and enhance operational efficiency.

Creating a Cohesive Experience

The design stage ensures that all elements of the event come together cohesively. From the visual aspects to the participant interactions, a well-designed event provides a seamless and integrated experience. This cohesiveness contributes to the overall success and positive perception of the event.

Adapting to Audience Preferences

Through research and understanding of the target audience, the design stage adapts the event to meet the preferences and expectations of attendees. This audience-centric approach increases the likelihood of a favorable response and ensures that the event resonates with its intended audience.

Design Approach

Designing a MICE event involves a thoughtful and strategic approach. Here are key steps and considerations for effective event design.

Understand the Event Objectives

Begin by understanding the overarching objectives of the event. What do you want to achieve? This understanding will guide the design process and ensure that every element contributes to the event's goals.

Translate Research Insights

Utilize insights gathered during the research stage to inform the design process. Consider the preferences, expectations, and demographic details of the target audience. Translate these insights into design elements that resonate with attendees.

Develop a Compelling Event Theme

The event theme serves as the central narrative and should encapsulate the essence of the occasion. Work collaboratively to develop a theme that aligns with the objectives and creates a memorable and cohesive experience.

Create a Strong Visual Identity

Design a visually compelling identity for the event, including logos, color schemes, and branding materials. Ensure consistency across all promotional materials, both online and offline. A strong visual identity reinforces the event's brand and helps with recognition.

Structure the Event Program

Collaborate with content creators and planners to structure the event program and agenda. Determine the sequence of activities, allocate time for key elements, and ensure a balanced mix of sessions. Consider the flow of the event to maximize participant engagement.

Plan the Event Space

The physical environment plays a crucial role in the overall experience. Plan the event space to align with the chosen theme and facilitate interactions. Consider factors such as seating arrangements, lighting, signage, and interactive elements that enhance engagement.

Design Event Collateral

Develop collateral such as brochures, signage, and digital assets that align with the established visual identity. These materials should not only convey essential information about the event but also contribute to the overall aesthetic and branding.

Incorporate Interactive Elements

Enhance participant engagement by incorporating interactive elements into the design. This could include networking zones, interactive displays, or technology-driven experiences. Interactive elements contribute to a dynamic and participatory event environment.

Consider Accessibility

Ensure that the event design is accessible to all participants. Consider factors such as venue accessibility, inclusive design for materials, and accommodations for individuals with diverse needs. A thoughtful approach to accessibility enhances the overall attendee experience.

Test and Iterate

Before the event, conduct tests and walkthroughs to ensure that the design elements work seamlessly. Gather feedback from stakeholders and make any necessary adjustments. An iterative approach allows for refinement and improvement.

Stay Current with Design Trends

Stay abreast of current design trends and technologies. Integrating innovative design elements can bring a fresh and contemporary feel to the event, keeping it dynamic and engaging.

Collaborate Effectively

Design is a collaborative process. Ensure effective communication and collaboration between designers, planners, content creators, and other stakeholders. Regular meetings and clear communication channels help keep everyone aligned with the design vision.

By following these steps and considerations, event organizers can design a MICE event that not only looks visually appealing but also contributes to a cohesive, engaging, and purposeful experience for attendees.

PLANNING: At a glance

☐ Purpose

Organize and coordinate all aspects of the event

Ensuring that it aligns with the established objectives

☐ Activities

Developing a Project Plan

Budget Allocation and Management

Venue Selection and Contract Negotiation

Vendor and Supplier Coordination

Logistics and Operations Planning

Risk Management and Contingency Planning

Team Coordination and Assigning Roles

☐ Outcome

A comprehensive and detailed plan

☐ Challenges and Considerations

Time Constraints

Changing Circumstances

☐ Tips for Success

Regular Communication

Continuous Monitoring

Contingency Plans

Team Training

The planning stage in MICE management is a critical phase

where the conceptualized vision of an event transforms into a detailed, actionable plan. This stage serves as the backbone of the entire process, focusing on meticulous organization and coordination to ensure that the event aligns with its objectives, stays within budget, and runs smoothly.

One of the primary activities during the planning stage is the development of a comprehensive project plan. This plan serves as a detailed roadmap, outlining tasks, milestones, and deadlines from pre-event preparations to post-event wrap-up. It provides a structured framework for the entire event team to follow, facilitating efficient execution and coordination.

Budget allocation and management are paramount during the planning stage. Organizers must carefully allocate resources across various aspects of the event, including venue rental, catering, technology, marketing, and personnel. Effective budget management is crucial for ensuring the financial viability of the event and successful execution within established constraints.

Venue selection and contract negotiation are key components of the planning process. Based on research and design requirements, organizers identify a suitable venue that aligns with the event's objectives and audience size. Successful negotiation of contracts with the venue ensures favorable terms and conditions that meet both budgetary and logistical considerations.

Vendor and supplier coordination is another critical activity during the planning stage. Organizers identify and collaborate with external contributors, such as catering services, audiovisual equipment providers, decorators, and logistics partners. This coordination is essential to guarantee that all external elements align seamlessly with the event's requirements and timeline.

Detailed logistics and operations planning contribute to the overall success of the event. This involves meticulous planning of participant registration, transportation, on-site security, and equipment setup. A well-organized logistics plan ensures a smooth and efficient flow of activities during the event.

Risk management and contingency planning are integral aspects of the planning stage. Organizers identify potential risks that could impact the event and develop contingency plans to address unforeseen challenges. This proactive approach minimizes disruptions and enhances the event's resilience in the face of unexpected situations.

Team coordination and role assignments play a crucial role in successful event planning. Clearly defining roles and responsibilities ensures that all team members are aligned with their tasks, contributing to a cohesive and efficient planning process.

In conclusion, the planning stage in MICE management yields a comprehensive and detailed plan that serves as the foundation for the successful execution of the event. From project plans to budget management, venue selection, vendor coordination, logistics planning, and risk management, each facet of the planning stage contributes to the seamless orchestration of a memorable and impactful event.

Why Planning

The planning stage is essential in MICE management because it lays the groundwork for a successful event. From strategic planning to resource allocation, risk management, and team coordination, this stage ensures that the event is well organized, financially viable, and capable of delivering a positive and impactful experience for all stakeholders involved.

Strategic Blueprint

The planning stage transforms the conceptualized vision of the event into a strategic blueprint. It involves the development of a comprehensive project plan that outlines tasks, timelines, and responsibilities. This plan serves as a roadmap for the entire event, providing a structured framework for execution.

Resource Allocation and Budget Management

Effective planning involves meticulous allocation of resources and budget management. Organizers need to allocate financial resources across various aspects of the event, such as venue, catering, technology, marketing, and personnel. Successful budget management ensures financial viability and prevents overspending.

Venue Selection and Contract Negotiation

During the planning stage, organizers select a suitable venue based on research and design requirements. Negotiating contracts with the venue is a critical aspect, ensuring that terms and conditions are favorable and align with the budget. The chosen venue sets the stage for the overall event experience.

Vendor and Supplier Coordination

Coordinating with vendors and suppliers is essential to ensure that external contributors align with the event's requirements and timeline. From catering services to audiovisual equipment providers, effective coordination enhances the quality and reliability of services.

Logistics and Operations Planning

Detailed logistics and operations planning contribute to the smooth execution of the event. This includes planning for participant registration, transportation, on-site security, and equipment setup. A well-organized logistics plan ensures that all elements come together seamlessly.

Risk Management and Contingency Planning

The planning stage involves identifying potential risks that could impact the event. Developing contingency plans allows organizers to address unforeseen challenges proactively. This risk management approach minimizes disruptions and enhances the event's overall resilience.

Team Coordination and Role Definition

Clear team coordination and role definition are critical for a successful event. The planning stage involves assigning roles and responsibilities to team members, ensuring that everyone is aligned with their tasks. Effective team coordination contributes to a cohesive and efficient planning process.

Efficient Use of Time

Time is a precious resource in event planning. The planning stage ensures efficient use of time by setting deadlines, milestones, and timelines for each aspect of the event. Proactive time management is crucial to avoid last-minute complications and ensure a well-organized event.

Quality Control

Planning serves as a mechanism for quality control throughout the event management process. By detailing every aspect in advance, organizers can ensure that each element meets the desired standards and contributes to the overall success of the event.

Customer Satisfaction

A well-planned event is more likely to meet or exceed participant expectations. Attendees benefit from a seamless experience, timely sessions, and well-organized logistics. Customer satisfaction is crucial for the success of the event and for building a positive reputation.

Planning Approach

Planning a MICE event involves a systematic and comprehensive approach. Here are key steps and considerations for effective event planning.

Define Clear Objectives

Clearly articulate the objectives of the event. What do you aim to achieve? Whether it's knowledge transfer, networking, or brand promotion, having well-defined objectives provides a guiding framework for the entire planning process.

Create a Detailed Project Plan

Develop a comprehensive project plan that outlines all tasks, milestones, and deadlines. Break down the planning process into manageable stages, ensuring that each aspect is covered, from pre-event preparations to post-event evaluations.

Allocate Budget Resources

Allocate financial resources across various components of the event. This includes venue rental, catering, technology, marketing, and personnel. Establishing a clear budget and managing it effectively is essential for financial viability.

Venue Selection and Contract Negotiation

Based on research and design requirements, choose a venue that aligns with the event's objectives and audience size. Negotiate contracts with the venue to secure favorable terms and conditions, including logistics, costs, and any additional services.

Vendor and Supplier Coordination

Identify and coordinate with vendors and suppliers for services such as catering, audiovisual equipment, decor, and logistics. Clearly communicate your requirements, expectations, and timelines to ensure that external contributors align seamlessly with the event's needs.

Logistics and Operations Planning

Develop detailed plans for logistics and operations, covering participant registration, transportation, on-site security, and equipment setup. A well-organized logistics plan contributes to the smooth execution of the event and enhances the overall participant experience.

Risk Management and Contingency Planning

Identify potential risks that could impact the event, ranging from technical glitches to unforeseen weather conditions. Develop contingency plans to address these risks proactively, minimizing disruptions and ensuring the event's resilience.

Team Coordination and Role Definition

Clearly define roles and responsibilities for team members involved in the planning process. Effective team coordination ensures that everyone understands their tasks and contributes to a cohesive and efficient planning process.

Utilize Event Planning Tools

Leverage event planning tools and software to streamline the process. Project management tools, budgeting software, and communication platforms can enhance organization, collaboration, and efficiency.

Regular Communication

Maintain open and regular communication channels within the planning team and with external stakeholders. Regular check-ins, updates, and feedback sessions contribute to effective collaboration and a shared understanding of progress.

Continuous Monitoring and Adaptation

Regularly monitor progress against the project plan and make adjustments as needed. An adaptive approach allows for continuous improvement and ensures that the planning process remains aligned with changing circumstances.

Engage Stakeholders

Involve key stakeholders, including sponsors, partners, and participants, throughout the planning process. Regularly update them on progress and seek input to ensure that their expectations align with the evolving plans.

Document and Evaluate

Document all planning decisions, contracts, and agreements. After the event, conduct a comprehensive evaluation to assess the success of the planning process and identify areas for improvement in future events.

By following these steps and considerations, event planners can create a robust and effective plan for MICE events. Thorough planning contributes to the success of the event, ensures a positive participant experience, and sets the stage for future events.

PROMOTION: At a glance

☐ Purpose

Market the event to the target audience, stakeholders, and potential participants

☐ Activities

Developing a Marketing Strategy

Utilizing Online and Offline Channels

Social Media Promotion/ Email Marketing Campaigns

Content Marketing/ Collaborating with Influencers

Creating Promotional Collateral

Early Bird and Special Offers/ Engaging Partners and Sponsors

☐ Outcome

A heightened awareness of the event

Increasing interest from the target audience

Growing number of registrations.

☐ Challenges and Considerations

Saturated Market/ Communication Consistency

Budget Constraints

☐ Tips for Success

Segment Your Audience/ Utilize Data Analytics

Create Engaging Content

The promotion stage in MICE management is a pivotal phase designed to elevate awareness, generate interest, and drive attendance for the upcoming event. At its core, the purpose is to effectively market the event to the target audience, stakeholders, and potential participants, ensuring a strong turnout and maximizing the impact of the event.

One of the primary activities during the promotion stage is the development of a comprehensive marketing strategy. This strategy serves as a roadmap, delineating the identification of target audiences, selection of promotional channels, and crafting key messages that communicate the value and benefits of attending the event.

The utilization of both online and offline promotional channels is a hallmark of a well-rounded promotion strategy. Leveraging the power of social media platforms, event organizers create engaging content that includes event highlights, speaker profiles, and behind-the-scenes glimpses. The goal is to foster a sense of community and excitement surrounding the event, encouraging participants to share their experiences.

Email marketing campaigns play a crucial role in maintaining ongoing communication throughout the promotional period. By segmenting the audience based on their interests and sending personalized invitations and updates, organizers can create a direct and targeted approach to potential attendees.

Content marketing becomes a valuable tool during the promotion stage. Compelling content related to the event theme, topics, and speakers is developed and shared across various platforms. Blog posts, articles, infographics, and videos contribute to positioning the event as a valuable and educational experience.

Collaborating with influencers or thought leaders in the industry is another effective strategy. Their endorsement and promotion significantly enhance the credibility and reach of the event. Influencers can share their unique perspective on the event, encouraging their followers to participate.

Designing and distributing promotional collateral, including brochures, flyers, and digital assets, is essential. Consistent branding across these materials reinforces the event identity and ensures that key information about the event, such as speakers, agenda, and registration details, is effectively communicated.

Encouraging early registration through special incentives, such as early bird discounts or exclusive access, creates a sense of urgency and drives early commitments. Engaging partners and sponsors in cross-promotion activities utilizes their networks and resources to reach a broader audience, enhancing the event's visibility.

In conclusion, the promotion stage is a dynamic and multifaceted process that aims to create anticipation, engage the audience, and drive participation. A successful promotion stage results in heightened awareness, increased interest, and a growing number of registrations, laying the foundation for a vibrant and impactful MICE event.

Why Promotion

The promotion stage is a cornerstone of MICE management, influencing attendance, reputation, and overall event success. By strategically promoting the event through diverse channels and engaging activities, organizers set the stage for a dynamic, well-attended, and impactful experience for participants and stakeholders alike.

Audience Awareness

The promotion stage serves as a vehicle for creating widespread awareness about the upcoming event. By effectively marketing the event to the target audience, organizers ensure that potential participants are informed about the event's existence, purpose, and value.

Generating Interest and Excitement

Promotion is the catalyst for generating interest and excitement surrounding the event. Engaging promotional activities, such as social media campaigns, influencer endorsements, and compelling content, create a buzz that captivates the audience and stimulates curiosity.

Maximizing Attendance

The ultimate goal of the promotion stage is to maximize attendance. By reaching a broader audience and convincing potential participants of the event's value proposition, organizers increase the likelihood of a strong turnout. A well-executed promotion strategy contributes to a vibrant and well-attended event.

Enhancing Event Reputation

Effective promotion contributes to building and enhancing the reputation of the event. Through consistent messaging, engaging content, and positive endorsements, the event becomes associated with quality and relevance, attracting participants who view it as a must-attend occasion.

Optimizing Return on Investment (ROI)

Successful promotion maximizes the return on investment for the event. Higher attendance levels mean increased opportunities for networking, knowledge transfer, and business interactions. This, in turn, contributes to the overall success and impact of the event.

Building Community and Engagement

Promotion fosters a sense of community and engagement among potential attendees. Social media platforms, influencer collaborations, and interactive content encourage participants to connect with each other before the event, creating a vibrant and participatory community.

Encouraging Early Commitments

Promotional strategies often include incentives for early registration, such as early bird discounts or exclusive access. This encourages participants to commit early, providing organizers with valuable insights into attendance numbers and allowing for better event planning.

Attracting Sponsorship and Partnerships

A well-promoted event attracts sponsors and partners who see value in reaching the event's audience. Increased visibility and a positive reputation make the event an attractive platform for organizations seeking exposure and engagement within the target industry.

Differentiating in a Crowded Market

In competitive industries, effective promotion is essential for differentiating the event from others in the market. Unique value propositions and compelling messaging help the event stand out, ensuring that it captures the attention of the target audience amid a crowded landscape.

Facilitating Post-Event Success

The success of the event extends beyond the actual dates. A well-promoted event leaves a lasting impression, contributing to positive post-event outcomes. Attendees are more likely to share their experiences, provide positive feedback, and contribute to the event's ongoing success.

Promotion Approach

Promoting an event effectively involves a combination of strategic planning, utilizing various channels, and engaging with the target audience. Here are key strategies and considerations for promoting an event.

Develop a Comprehensive Marketing Plan

Start by creating a detailed marketing plan that outlines your promotional strategy. Define your target audience, key messaging, promotional channels, and a timeline for different activities. A well-thought-out plan provides a roadmap for the entire promotion process.

Leverage Social Media Platforms

Utilize the power of social media to connect with your audience. Create dedicated event pages, share engaging content, and use targeted advertisements to reach a broader audience. Encourage participants to share their excitement and experiences, creating a social media buzz.

Email Marketing Campaigns

Design targeted email-marketing campaigns to reach potential attendees. Segment your email list based on interests and preferences, and send-personalized invitations, updates, and reminders. Email campaigns are effective for maintaining ongoing communication throughout the promotional period.

Create Compelling Content

Develop high quality and compelling content related to the event. This can include blog posts, articles, infographics, videos, and podcasts. Share this content across various platforms to position the event as a valuable and educational experience.

Collaborate with Influencers and Partners

Identify and collaborate with influencers or thought leaders in your industry. Their endorsement and promotion can significantly enhance the credibility and reach of your event. Engage event partners to cross-promote, leveraging each other's networks and resources.

Utilize Event Websites and Online Platforms

Create a dedicated event website or utilize online platforms that cater to event promotion. Include detailed information about the event, registration details, speakers, and agenda. Optimize the website for search engines to enhance its visibility.

Offer Early Bird and Special Incentives

Encourage early registration by offering special incentives, such as early bird discounts, exclusive access, or limited-time offers. Creating a sense of urgency can drive early commitments and boost overall registration numbers.

Employ Paid Advertising

Consider using paid advertising channels such as Google Ads or social media advertisements. Target specific demographics and interests to reach individuals who are likely to be interested in your event. Monitor and optimize your ad campaigns for maximum effectiveness.

Utilize Event Listings and Directories

List your event on relevant event directories and platforms. This increases the visibility of your event within the industry and makes it easier for potential attendees to find information and register.

Host Webinars or Pre-Event Virtual Sessions

Host webinars or virtual sessions leading up to the event. These can serve as teasers, providing a taste of what attendees can expect. It also creates opportunities for interaction and engagement before the main event.

Encourage Attendee Referrals

Implement a referral program where registered attendees are

incentivized to refer others to the event. Word-of-mouth recommendations from satisfied participants can be a powerful promotion tool.

Utilize Traditional Marketing Channels

Don't overlook traditional marketing channels such as print materials, direct mail, and industry publications. Depending on your target audience, these channels can still be effective in reaching certain demographics.

Monitor and Analyze Results

Implement tracking mechanisms to monitor the effectiveness of different promotional channels. Analyze data regularly to understand what is working well and make adjustments accordingly. This data-driven approach ensures ongoing optimization of your promotion strategy.

By incorporating these strategies into your promotion plan, you can create a well-rounded and effective promotional campaign that reaches your target audience, generates interest, and drives attendance to your MICE event.

COORDINATION: At a glance

☐ **Purpose**

Ensure seamless coordination and implementation of all aspects outlined in the planning phase.

☐ **Activities**

Team Briefings and Assignments

Vendor and Supplier Coordination

Venue Setup and Logistics

Participant Registration and Welcoming

On-Site Technical Support/ Timeline Management:

Speaker and Presenter Coordination

Participant Engagement Activities

Catering and Hospitality Services:

Communication and Troubleshooting

☐ **Outcome**

An event that adheres to the established plan, with all elements working in harmony.

☐ **Challenges and Considerations**

Unforeseen Issues/ Communication Breakdowns

Vendor and Team Alignment

☐ **Tips for Success**

Pre-event Rehearsals/ Comprehensive Checklists

Continuous Monitoring

The coordination stage in MICE management marks the pivotal transition from meticulous planning to active execution. At its core, the purpose of this stage is to ensure the seamless coordination and implementation of all facets outlined during the planning phase. This involves bringing together diverse elements and stakeholders to execute the event according to the established plan, with a keen focus on achieving the envisioned objectives.

One of the foundational activities during the coordination stage is conducting team briefings and assignments. These sessions serve to align the event team, ensuring a clear understanding of roles and responsibilities. The coordination team assigns specific tasks and clarifies expectations, fostering a well-coordinated and cohesive effort for the successful execution of the event.

Close collaboration with vendors and suppliers is paramount during the coordination stage. Coordinators work diligently to ensure external partners are aligned with the event's requirements, confirming delivery schedules, set-up details, and any logistical considerations. Effective communication with external entities is crucial for the smooth coordination of various event components.

The coordination stage involves overseeing the physical setup of the event venue, including staging, seating arrangements, audiovisual equipment, and signage. Coordinators work hand-in-hand with venue staff to guarantee that all logistical aspects are meticulously addressed, creating an environment ready to welcome participants.

A key focus during the coordination stage is participant registration and welcoming. Coordinators implement processes that ensure a smooth and efficient check-in experience, providing clear signage and staff assistance to guide attendees. This initial welcoming process sets the tone for a positive and engaging participant experience.

On-site technical support is a critical aspect of coordination, addressing audiovisual setups, lighting, and any technological requirements. Coordinators ensure the presence of a technical support team to promptly handle any issues, guaranteeing that presentations and sessions run seamlessly.

A comprehensive timeline is maintained during the coordination stage to manage the flow of activities throughout the event. This includes sessions, breaks, and networking opportunities. Proactive timeline management is crucial for keeping the event on track and ensuring a well-organized and engaging experience for participants.

Coordination extends to speaker and presenter management, involving confirmation of availability, arrival times, and any specific requirements. Coordinators work to ensure that presentation materials are ready and that speakers are familiar with the event agenda, contributing to the overall success of sessions.

The successful execution of engagement activities is coordinated to keep participants actively involved and connected throughout the event. This may include networking sessions, interactive discussions, and entertainment, enhancing the overall participant experience and contributing to the event's success.

Coordination also encompasses catering services and hospitality arrangements. Coordinators work closely to ensure that food and beverages are provided according to the agreed-upon menu and schedule. Attention to hospitality services, including VIP arrangements, enhances the overall participant experience.

Effective communication channels are established during the coordination stage for the event team to address any issues or changes promptly. Coordinators anticipate potential challenges and have contingency plans in place, ensuring effective troubleshooting and a seamless event experience.

The coordination stage is the linchpin of MICE management, where meticulous planning transforms into active execution.

Successful coordination results in the seamless operation of the event, with all elements working harmoniously to create a memorable and impactful experience for participants and stakeholders alike.

Why Coordination

The coordination stage is indispensable in MICE management because it ensures the effective translation of plans into action, leading to a successful event that meets objectives, satisfies stakeholders, and leaves a positive and enduring impact on participants and the broader industry.

Seamless Execution

The coordination stage is the critical juncture where plans transition into action. Successful coordination ensures that all elements of the event are executed seamlessly, contributing to a smooth and well-organized experience for participants.

Participant Experience

A well-coordinated event directly influences the participant experience. From registration to sessions, networking, and engagement activities, effective coordination enhances the overall experience, leaving a positive and lasting impression on attendees.

Stakeholder Satisfaction

Stakeholders, including sponsors, partners, and organizers, have invested time and resources in the event's success. The coordination stage plays a pivotal role in delivering on their expectations, leading to stakeholder satisfaction and fostering ongoing support.

Risk Mitigation

Effective coordination involves anticipating potential challenges and having contingency plans in place. This proactive approach to risk mitigation minimizes disruptions and ensures that any issues that arise during the event are addressed promptly and efficiently.

Achieving Objectives

Events are typically organized with specific objectives in mind, whether it's knowledge transfer, networking, or brand promotion. The coordination stage is instrumental in translating these objectives into tangible outcomes, aligning the execution with the intended goals.

Timely Execution

Maintaining a detailed timeline during the coordination stage is crucial for ensuring that activities progress according to schedule. Timely execution is vital for keeping the event on track, preventing delays, and optimizing the use of time and resources.

Professional Image

A well-coordinated event projects a professional image to participants, stakeholders, and the industry at large. It reflects organizational competence and dedication to delivering a high-quality experience, contributing to a positive reputation.

Adaptability to Changes

Events are dynamic, and unforeseen changes can occur. The coordination stage's importance lies in the ability to adapt to these changes efficiently. Coordinators must be responsive and make informed decisions to address unexpected situations.

Resource Optimization

Efficient coordination contributes to the optimal use of resources, including personnel, equipment, and budget. Maximizing resource utilization ensures that the event is cost-effective while still delivering a high-quality experience.

Enhanced Communication

Clear and effective communication is a cornerstone of successful coordination. Participants, team members, and external partners rely on efficient communication channels during the event. Well-established communication contributes to a cohesive and informed team.

Post-Event Evaluation

The success of an event is often evaluated post-execution. A well-coordinated event provides a solid foundation for positive evaluations, feedback, and insights. This information is valuable for organizers to assess what worked well and identify areas for improvement in future events.

Legacy and Reputation

The coordination stage contributes to the legacy of the event and the organization's overall reputation. A successfully coordinated event becomes part of the organization's record of accomplishment, influencing future partnerships, sponsorships, and participant trust.

Coordination Approach

Effectively coordinating an event involves adopting strategic approaches that facilitate seamless execution and collaboration among various stakeholders. Here are key approaches to coordination.

Comprehensive Planning

Begin with a comprehensive and detailed planning phase. Clearly outline roles, responsibilities, timelines, and dependencies. A well-thought-out plan serves as the foundation for successful coordination.

Establish a Centralized Communication Hub

Create a centralized communication hub, such as a digital platform or project management tool, to facilitate communication among team members, vendors, and stakeholders. This ensures that everyone is on the same page and has access to real-time information.

Pre-event Rehearsals and Briefings

Conduct pre-event rehearsals and briefings to ensure that everyone involved understands their roles and responsibilities. This includes event team members, speakers, vendors, and volunteers. Practice sessions help identify and address potential issues before the actual event.

Cross-functional Coordination

Foster cross-functional coordination by establishing clear communication channels between different teams and departments involved in the event. Regular check-ins and updates ensure that everyone is aligned with the overarching goals and timelines.

Vendor and Supplier Collaboration

Establish strong collaboration with vendors and suppliers. Clearly communicate expectations, deliverables, and timelines. Regular check-ins and site visits can enhance coordination, particularly when it comes to venue setup, catering, and technical support.

Real-time Communication Channels

Implement real-time communication channels, such as instant messaging or walkie-talkie systems, to address immediate needs and changes during the event. Quick and efficient communication is crucial for resolving issues on the spot.

Delegate and Empower

Delegate tasks and empower team members to make informed decisions within their areas of responsibility. A decentralized decision-making approach allows for more agile responses to challenges as they arise.

Timeline Management

Maintain a detailed timeline and schedule for all activities during the event. Use tools and visuals to communicate the timeline to the entire team. Timely execution of activities is key to preventing bottlenecks and ensuring a smooth flow of the event.

Contingency Planning

Develop robust contingency plans for potential disruptions. Anticipate common issues that may arise during events and outline clear steps for resolution. Having contingency plans in place enables quick responses to unforeseen challenges.

Technology Integration

Leverage technology to streamline coordination processes. Event management software, communication apps, and project management tools can enhance collaboration and organization. Choose tools that align with the specific needs of your event.

Regular Check-ins and Updates

Schedule regular check-ins and updates with the entire team. These sessions provide opportunities to address concerns, share progress, and make any necessary adjustments to the plan. Open communication contributes to a cohesive and well-coordinated effort.

Post-event Debriefing

Conduct a thorough post-event debriefing session to gather feedback from team members and stakeholders. Evaluate what worked well, identify areas for improvement, and document lessons learned. This information is invaluable for refining coordination strategies in future events.

Continuous Improvement

Adopt a mindset of continuous improvement. Regularly assess the effectiveness of coordination processes and seek feedback from team members and participants. Use insights gained from each event to enhance coordination practices for future endeavors.

By integrating these approaches into the coordination stage, event organizers can foster a collaborative and agile environment, ensuring the successful execution of MICE events. Effective coordination contributes to a positive participant experience, stakeholder satisfaction, and the overall success and reputation of the event.

EVALUATION: At a glance

☐ **Purpose**

Gather insights that can inform future event planning and improve the overall effectiveness of MICE initiatives.

☐ **Activities**

Objective Assessment/ Participant Feedback Surveys

Stakeholder Feedback/ Financial Evaluation

Post-event Analytics/ Speaker and Session Evaluations

Logistical Review/ Compliance and Risk Assessment

Post-event Reports

☐ **Outcome**

A thorough understanding of the event's strengths, weaknesses, and overall impact.

☐ **Challenges and Considerations**

Subjectivity of Feedback/ Timely Data Collection

Balancing Quantitative and Qualitative Data

☐ **Tips for Success**

Use Diverse Evaluation Methods/ Compare against Benchmarks

Engage in Continuous Improvement

☐ **Key Questions to Answer**

 - What aspects of the event did participants find most valuable?

 - What are the key takeaways from the event, including
   successes and areas for improvement?

The evaluation stage, the culmination of the MICE (Meetings, Incentives, Conferences, and Exhibitions/Events) management process, holds the pivotal role of assessing the event's overall success and gathering insights for future improvements.

This phase begins with a thorough examination of participant feedback, a key metric for understanding the event's impact. Organizers seek answers to questions such as what participants found most valuable, their satisfaction with the content, and their overall experience, encompassing logistics and engagement opportunities. This firsthand feedback provides a nuanced perspective on the event's strengths and areas for enhancement, directly from those who experienced it.

Parallel to gauging participant experiences, the financial evaluation delves into the fiscal aspects of the event. Organizers scrutinize the alignment of actual expenses with the budget, identifying any unexpected costs. Equally crucial is assessing the return on investment (ROI) for sponsors, exhibitors, and the organizing entity. These financial insights not only offer a retrospective view of the event's financial health but also inform future budgeting strategies for subsequent MICE initiatives.

The capstone of the evaluation stage involves synthesizing insights from participant feedback, financial evaluations, and various other assessments into comprehensive post-event reports. These reports distill key takeaways, successes, and areas for improvement. Comparisons against benchmarks or industry standards offer valuable context. The culmination of these findings results in actionable recommendations that serve as a roadmap for refining strategies and ensuring continuous improvement in future MICE endeavors.

In essence, the evaluation stage serves as the compass for navigating the dynamic landscape of MICE management. By systematically addressing participant experiences, financial performance, and overarching lessons learned, organizers gain a holistic understanding of the event's impact, paving the way for elevated success in subsequent MICE initiatives.

Why Evaluation

The evaluation stage is integral to the success and longevity of MICE events. It serves as a compass for improvement, a tool for accountability, and a mechanism for staying attuned to participant and industry needs. The insights gained from this stage are not only valuable for the individual event but also contribute to the growth and evolution of the broader MICE management landscape.

Informing Future Decision-Making

The evaluation stage provides critical insights that inform future decision-making. By assessing the event's successes and areas for improvement, organizers can make informed choices, refine strategies, and enhance the effectiveness of future MICE initiatives.

Continuous Improvement

Evaluation fosters a culture of continuous improvement. By analyzing participant feedback, financial performance, and overall outcomes, organizers identify opportunities for refinement. This iterative process ensures that each subsequent event builds upon the lessons learned, delivering an increasingly impactful experience.

Demonstrating Accountability

Through financial evaluations and transparent reporting, the evaluation stage demonstrates accountability to stakeholders, sponsors, and partners. Organizers can showcase how resources were utilized, the ROI achieved, and the steps taken to address any challenges. This transparency enhances trust and strengthens relationships with stakeholders.

Enhancing Participant Satisfaction

Participant feedback is a cornerstone of the evaluation stage. Understanding what worked well and areas that need improvement enables organizers to enhance participant satisfaction. This, in turn, contributes to positive word-of-mouth, increased attendance in future events, and a favorable reputation within the industry.

Optimizing Resource Allocation

Financial evaluations during the evaluation stage contribute to optimizing resource allocation. By scrutinizing actual expenses and ROI, organizers can identify areas where resources were efficiently utilized and pinpoint opportunities for cost-effectiveness in future events.

Setting Benchmarks for Success

Evaluation sets benchmarks for success. By comparing outcomes against predefined objectives and industry standards, organizers gain a clear understanding of the event's performance. This benchmarking process helps establish realistic goals for future events and enables organizers to measure success in a meaningful context.

Adapting to Industry Trends

The MICE industry is dynamic, and staying abreast of industry trends is crucial for relevance and competitiveness. The evaluation stage provides an opportunity to assess how well the event aligns with current trends and audience preferences, enabling organizers to adapt strategies accordingly.

Facilitating Stakeholder Engagement

Stakeholders, including sponsors, exhibitors, and partners, invest in events with specific expectations. The evaluation stage allows organizers to gauge the satisfaction of stakeholders and understand how well these expectations were met. Positive stakeholder experiences contribute to ongoing support and engagement in future events.

Learning from Challenges

Not every event unfolds without challenges. The evaluation stage is a platform for learning from these challenges. By conducting a thorough review of logistical issues, compliance concerns, or unforeseen obstacles, organizers can develop strategies to address similar challenges in the future.

Strategic Planning and Innovation

Evaluation provides a foundation for strategic planning and innovation. Organizers can identify areas where innovation is needed, whether in event formats, technology integration, or engagement strategies. This forward-looking approach positions events as dynamic and responsive to changing industry landscapes.

Evaluation Approach

Evaluating MICE events requires a comprehensive approach that considers various aspects of the event's objectives, execution, and impact. Here are key approaches and methods to effectively evaluate MICE events.

Participant Feedback Surveys

Implementing participant feedback surveys is a fundamental method for gathering insights directly from attendees. Surveys can cover topics such as session content, speaker effectiveness, logistics, and overall satisfaction.

Use post-event surveys distributed electronically to capture a broad range of opinions. Ensure the survey design includes both quantitative (rating scales) and qualitative (open-ended questions) components for a thorough assessment.

Stakeholder Interviews and Feedback

Conducting one-on-one interviews with key stakeholders, including sponsors, partners, and exhibitors, offers a personalized and in-depth understanding of their perspectives. Schedule post-event interviews to discuss their experiences, expectations, and areas for improvement. This approach fosters open communication and strengthens future collaborations.

Financial Evaluation and ROI Analysis

Analyzing the financial aspects of the event provides insights into budget adherence, revenue generation, and return on investment (ROI) for sponsors and organizers. Review budget versus actual expenditures, assess revenue streams, and calculate ROI. This financial evaluation helps identify cost-effective strategies and areas for optimization in future events.

Quantitative Data Analytics

Utilizing data analytics tools provides quantitative insights into various event metrics, such as attendance rates, session engagement, and social media impressions. Integrate analytics platforms to track and analyze key performance indicators (KPIs). This approach supplements qualitative feedback with data-driven insights, offering a more comprehensive view of the event's impact.

Post-event Reports and Documentation

Compiling post-event reports consolidates findings from different evaluation methods into a comprehensive document. Develop detailed reports that summarize participant feedback, financial outcomes, analytics data, and stakeholder perspectives. These reports serve as valuable references for future planning and organizational learning.

Logistical and Operational Review

Evaluating the logistical and operational aspects of the event involves reviewing venue setup, registration processes, and overall event flow. Conduct a detailed post-event review of logistical processes, identifying any challenges or areas for improvement. This hands-on approach ensures a practical understanding of operational successes and pain points.

Comparisons against Benchmarks and Industry Standards

Benchmarking involves comparing the event's outcomes against predefined objectives and industry standards. Establish benchmarks during the planning phase and use them as reference points during the evaluation. Assess how well the event performed relative to these benchmarks, identifying areas of success and opportunities for growth.

SWOT Analysis (Strengths, Weaknesses, Opportunities, Threats)

Conducting a SWOT analysis provides a structured framework for evaluating internal and external factors that impact the event's success. Identify strengths, weaknesses, opportunities, and threats related to the event. This strategic analysis helps organizers leverage strengths, address weaknesses, capitalize on opportunities, and mitigate potential threats.

Compliance and Risk Assessment

Evaluate the event's compliance with regulations and conduct a risk assessment to identify areas of vulnerability. Review regulatory compliance, safety protocols, and risk management strategies. This approach ensures that the event adheres to legal standards and is well-prepared to address potential risks in the future.

Post-event Debriefing Sessions

Facilitate debriefing sessions with the organizing team to discuss the event's successes, challenges, and areas for improvement. Schedule a debriefing meeting shortly after the event to capture fresh insights. Encourage open communication and collaboration among team members, fostering a culture of continuous improvement.

Technology Integration Assessment

Evaluate the effectiveness of technology integration during the event, including event management software, mobile apps, and virtual elements. Gather feedback on technology usage, assess user experiences, and identify areas for enhancement. This approach ensures that technology aligns with participant expectations and enhances overall event effectiveness.

By adopting a multifaceted approach that combines these evaluation methods, organizers can gather comprehensive insights into the various facets of MICE events. This holistic evaluation contributes to a more nuanced understanding of the event's success, challenges, and opportunities for improvement, ultimately guiding strategic decisions for future initiatives.

Review Quiz

1. Research Stage

What is the primary purpose of the research stage in MICE management?

a. Event execution

b. Participant engagement

c. Gathering insights for decision-making

d. Budget planning

2. Design Stage

During the design stage, what is a key consideration for organizers?

a. Post-event evaluations

b. Selecting the event date

c. Coordination with vendors

d. Identifying event objectives and activities

3. Planning Stage

Why is the planning stage considered crucial in MICE management?

a. To gather participant feedback

b. To assess financial performance

c. To ensure seamless execution

d. To conduct risk assessments

4. Promotion Stage

What is a primary activity during the promotion stage?

a. On-site coordination

b. Evaluating participant feedback

c. Marketing and advertising

d. Vendor collaboration

5. Coordination Stage

What is a primary responsibility during the coordination stage?

a. Setting event objectives

b. Conducting pre-event research

c. Overseeing event logistics

d. Financial analysis

6. Evaluation Stage

What is a key outcome of the evaluation stage in MICE management?

a. Setting benchmarks for success

b. Selecting event dates

c. Conducting risk assessments

d. Designing promotional materials

Discussion Topic

Planning a Sustainable Campus Networking Event

Guidelines

① Introduction

Start the session by introducing the concept of event planning and its relevance in various fields. Emphasize the importance of sustainability in contemporary event management.

② Selecting the Event Type

Discuss various types of events suitable for a university campus (e.g., career fair, networking mixer, workshop). Encourage participants to consider the goals of the event and its alignment with sustainability principles.

③ Identifying Objectives

Have participants brainstorm and articulate clear objectives for the event. Examples may include fostering connections, promoting sustainability initiatives, or providing learning opportunities.

④ Research and Design

Break the participants into smaller groups or individuals and assign each group or each one a specific aspect of the event (e.g., venue selection, thematic design, catering). Participants research and design their assigned aspect, ensuring it aligns with sustainability goals.

⑤ Planning and Coordination

Bring the groups back together and have them share their research and designs. Discuss the importance of effective planning, including logistics, timelines, and responsibilities.

Encourage discussions on how sustainability considerations can be integrated into various planning aspects.

⑥ Promotion and Outreach

Assign another task to the groups—planning the promotional and outreach activities for the event. Explore creative and sustainable promotional strategies, considering social media, campus channels, and collaboration with student organizations.

⑦ Budgeting and Resource Allocation

Discuss the financial aspects of event planning, emphasizing the importance of budgeting and resource optimization. Encourage participants to explore cost-effective and sustainable options for various event components.

⑧ Group Presentation

Each group presents its planned aspects of the event, emphasizing sustainability considerations. Allow for questions and discussions after each presentation.

4. PROTOCOL IN MICE INDUSTRY

Understanding Protocols in MICE Industry

In a general sense, protocol refers to a set of rules or guidelines that dictate appropriate behavior in a given context. It is a structured system of formalities and customs that help regulate interactions, communication, and procedures. The origins of protocol can be traced back to diplomatic practices where it was used to govern official ceremonies, negotiations, and other interactions between representatives of different entities.

Protocol in the MICE industry refers to a set of established rules, guidelines, and formalities that govern behavior, communication, and procedures during meetings, incentives, conferences, and exhibitions. Rooted in the broader concept of diplomatic and organizational protocol, it encompasses a range of practices aimed at ensuring events are conducted smoothly, professionally, and in accordance with accepted standards and etiquette.

Understanding the purpose of protocol in the MICE industry is paramount to appreciating its multifaceted role. One of its primary functions is to maintain a high level of professionalism, not only in interactions between organizers but also in presentations and overall event execution. This commitment to professionalism contributes significantly to enhancing the image and reputation of the organizers, participants, and the event itself. Moreover, protocol plays a crucial role in facilitating smooth operations throughout the planning and execution of MICE events. By providing a structured framework, it minimizes misunderstandings and streamlines communication, ensuring that the diverse needs and expectations of participants, particularly in international settings, are met with cultural sensitivity and respect.

In the realm of security and safety, protocol establishes guidelines to ensure the well-being of all participants. From defining procedures for the treatment of VIPs to guiding effective communication practices, it encompasses a wide spectrum of considerations. Embracing technology, audiovisual equipment, and sustainable event management practices, protocol further contributes to the overall success and positive experience of MICE activities.

The role of protocol extends beyond mere guidelines; it is instrumental in establishing industry standards and best practices for conducting events. By doing so, it provides a consistent framework across different types of MICE activities, contributing to a positive and memorable experience for participants, attendees, and guests. Moreover, its role in mitigating risks, building trust, and adapting to diverse contexts underscores its significance in the ever-evolving landscape of the MICE industry.

As we navigate through the chapters of this book, it becomes evident that protocol is more than a set of rules; it is a guiding philosophy that ensures the professionalism, efficiency, and success of MICE events. Rooted in history and adapted to contemporary needs, protocol stands as an indispensable tool in the hands of event organizers, shaping the industry's future while honoring its past.

Key Differences between Protocol and Etiquette

In the realm of professional conduct and social interactions, two concepts play pivotal roles: protocol and etiquette. These terms, though related, carry distinct meanings and applications that merit exploration.

Protocol is a set of rules, guidelines, and formal procedures designed to govern behavior, communication, and procedures in specific contexts. Its formality and association with official or ceremonial occasions characterize it. Whether applied in diplomatic settings or the meticulously planned events of the MICE industry, protocol provides a structured framework to ensure order, efficiency, and adherence to established standards.

In contrast, etiquette encompasses socially accepted norms

and customs that guide behavior in various social situations. Unlike the explicit rules of protocol, etiquette is a collection of unwritten rules governing politeness, courtesy, and respect. It is versatile, finding application in both formal and informal settings, emphasizing everyday manners and considerations for others.

The distinction between these concepts becomes clearer when examining their formality and settings. Protocol, being more formal, is often linked to specific professional or official contexts. It dictates the order of events, the treatment of VIPs, and the use of technology during conferences in the MICE industry. On the other hand, etiquette is more broadly applicable, guiding individuals through a wide range of social situations, from formal gatherings to casual interactions.

While protocol involves explicit rules and procedures, etiquette is rooted in socially accepted norms and customs. Protocol often narrows its focus to specific procedures and hierarchical structures, such as those found in diplomatic engagements or large-scale events. In contrast, etiquette encompasses a broader spectrum, emphasizing behaviors related to politeness, respect, and consideration for others in everyday life.

Understanding these concepts is crucial in navigating professional and social landscapes. As we delve deeper into the chapters of this book, we will explore how protocol and etiquette shape our interactions, influence perceptions, and contribute to the overall fabric of human communication and behavior. Each concept, with its unique characteristics, plays a distinct yet complementary role in guiding individuals through the intricacies of diverse and dynamic social environments.

key differences between protocol and etiquette		
	Protocol	Etiquette
Definition	Set of rules and formal procedures.	Socially accepted norms and customs.
Formality	More formal, often associated with official settings.	Applies to both formal and informal settings.
Setting	Linked to specific professional or official contexts.	Applicable in a wide range of social situations.
Rules vs. Social Norms	Involves explicit rules and procedures.	Involves socially accepted norms and customs.
Scope	Can be narrowly focused on specific procedures and structures.	Encompasses a wider range of behaviors related to politeness, respect, and consideration.
Example	Dictates the order of events, VIP treatment in the MICE industry.	Involves how to greet someone, table manners, and responses to invitations.

Types of Protocols

In the dynamic world of the MICE industry, the implementation of protocols is crucial for the seamless orchestration of events. These protocols can be broadly categorized into two main groups: Organizational Protocols and Event-Specific Protocols.

Organizational Protocols encompass the internal workings of the event planning team. Internal Communication Protocols set the tone for effective team communication, ensuring a well-informed and cohesive group. Coordination Protocols, on the other hand, guide the collaboration between different teams involved in event planning, preventing overlaps and ensuring a streamlined process. Financial Protocols lay the groundwork for budgeting, financial approvals, and expense tracking, maintaining financial discipline and transparency. Lastly, Security and Emergency Protocols prioritize the safety of participants, offering clear guidelines for emergency response plans and security measures.

Turning our attention to Event-Specific Protocols, Registration and Check-In Protocols dictate the procedures for participant registration and check-in, guaranteeing a smooth start to the event. Speaker and Presentation Protocols set guidelines for managing speakers, presentations, and Q&A sessions. Networking Protocols facilitate meaningful connections among participants, providing structured networking opportunities. Technology Integration Protocols ensure the seamless use of technology, audiovisual equipment, and event apps. Environmental and Sustainability Protocols contribute to sustainability goals by incorporating eco-friendly practices into event planning. Cultural Sensitivity Protocols address diverse audiences' needs, preventing cultural misunderstandings. VIP and Dignitary Treatment Protocols outline the special accommodations and personalized services extended to high-profile guests, enhancing their overall experience.

These protocols collectively form a comprehensive framework that underpins the professionalism, efficiency, and positive experiences for all stakeholders involved in MICE events. As we delve into the specifics of each protocol, we gain insights into the intricacies of event planning that contribute to the success of these dynamic and impactful gatherings.

Event-Specific Protocols

Registration and Check-In Protocols

Event-Specific Protocols begin with Registration and Check-In, encompassing guidelines for the registration process, check-in procedures, and the distribution of event materials. This may involve leveraging online registration systems and on-site check-in protocols, ensuring a streamlined and efficient experience for participants. The significance of Registration and Check-In Protocols lies in guaranteeing a smooth and organized start to the event for participants. These protocols set the tone for attendee experience, minimizing wait times, reducing congestion, and fostering overall satisfaction. Effective Registration and Check-In Protocols involve a combination of pre-event online registration processes and on-site check-in procedures.

· Pre-Event Communication
· QR Code Check-In
· Express Check-In for VIPs
· On-Site Registration Stations

Speaker and Presentation Protocols

Speaker and Presentation Protocols encompass a set of guidelines and procedures designed to manage speakers and presentations effectively during events. This includes a comprehensive approach to speaker preparation, adherence to time limits, addressing audiovisual requirements, and facilitating engaging Q&A sessions. The importance of Speaker and Presentation Protocols lies in maintaining the quality and coherence of presentations throughout the event. Well-managed protocols ensure that speakers are well-prepared, presentations align with the overall schedule, and interactive elements such as Q&A sessions enhance audience engagement.

· Speaker Rehearsal
· Strict Time Management
· Audiovisual Coordination
· Interactive Q&A App

Networking Protocols
Networking Protocols involve the establishment of guidelines and procedures to facilitate meaningful networking opportunities during events. This encompasses various aspects, including the structure of networking sessions, designated areas for discussions, and methods for exchanging contact information.

The importance of Networking Protocols lies in creating an environment that fosters connections among participants. Well-designed protocols enhance the networking experience, contributing to the overall success of the event by promoting meaningful interactions and relationship building.

· Themed Networking Sessions

· Discussion Lounges

· Digital Business Cards

· Facilitated Networking Activities

Technology Integration Protocols

Technology Integration Protocols involve establishing guidelines and procedures for the seamless incorporation of technology into various aspects of the event. This includes the use of audiovisual equipment, event apps, interactive tools, and other technological features that enhance the overall event experience. The importance of Technology Integration Protocols lies in ensuring that technology enhances, rather than disrupts, the event experience. Well-defined protocols prevent technical glitches, improve participant engagement, and contribute to the overall success of the event.

· Event App Integration

· Pre-Event Technology Checks

· Interactive Presentation Tools

· Virtual Reality (VR) Exhibits

Environmental and Sustainability Protocols

Environmental and Sustainability Protocols involve the integration of environmentally friendly practices into various aspects of event planning and execution. This includes strategies to reduce waste, promote energy efficiency, and use sustainable materials, aligning the event with broader sustainability goals. The importance of Environmental and Sustainability Protocols lies in contributing to global sustainability efforts and demonstrating a commitment to responsible event management. These protocols not only minimize the environmental impact of the event but also resonate positively with environmentally conscious participants.

· Digital-Only Event Materials
· Reusable Name Badges
· Green Catering Practices
· Carbon Offset Initiatives

Cultural Sensitivity Protocols

Cultural Sensitivity Protocols involve the establishment of guidelines and procedures to ensure that event planning and execution are considerate of diverse cultural backgrounds. This includes addressing cultural nuances in catering, scheduling, communication, and other aspects to create an inclusive and respectful event environment. The importance of Cultural

Sensitivity Protocols lies in promoting inclusivity, avoiding cultural misunderstandings, and creating an environment where participants from diverse cultural backgrounds feel valued and respected. This contributes to a positive and harmonious event experience for all attendees.

· Diverse Menu Options
· Scheduling Considerations
· Multilingual Event Materials
· Cultural Sensitivity Guidelines

VIP and Dignitary Treatment Protocols

VIP and Dignitary Treatment Protocols involve the establishment of guidelines and procedures to ensure that high-profile guests, such as VIPs and dignitaries, receive personalized and exceptional treatment during the event. This includes special accommodations, dedicated services, and designated areas to enhance their overall experience. The importance of VIP and Dignitary Treatment Protocols lies in creating a positive and memorable experience for influential guests. These protocols not only contribute to the success of the event but also foster positive relationships, goodwill, and potential future collaborations.

- VIP Lounges
- Personalized Welcome Packages
- Dedicated Concierge Services
- Exclusive Access to Key Events

Courtesies and Hierarchical Arrangements

In the intricate tapestry of professional interactions, understanding and adhering to courtesies and hierarchical arrangements play pivotal roles in shaping the dynamics of engagements. From the nuanced art of greetings to the thoughtfully orchestrated seating protocols, these elements contribute significantly to the establishment of respect, harmony, and effective communication. This exploration delves into the essential facets of courtesies and hierarchical arrangements, shedding light on the protocols that govern various aspects of interpersonal engagements in both formal and informal settings.

Forms of Address
High-Ranking Officials: Address high-ranking officials, such as ambassadors or ministers, using their full titles and honorifics.
ex. Your Excellency or Minister [Last Name].
Middle-Ranking Officials: Use appropriate titles such as Mr., Mrs., or Ms. along with the official's last name.

Lower-Ranking Officials: Use standard titles and last names without additional honorifics.

Forms of Address	Calling Name
President Prime Minister	Mr./Madame President Prime Minister (Do not call their name)
Foreign Ambassador Minister Speaker of National Assembly	Mr./Madame Ambassador Mr. Minister Mr. Speaker
Senator Congressman Governor Mayor Vice Minister Level Officials	Representative(Surname) Governor(Surname) Mayor(Surname)

Source: 국제회의기획자와 국제교류담당자를 위한 실무노트, 이나현(BG북갤러리, 2018)

Seating Arrangement

Head of Delegation: The head of the delegation is typically seated in the central position, with other members arranged according to their hierarchical status.

Rank-Based Seating: Arrange seating based on the official's rank or position, with higher-ranking individuals given precedence.

Host-Guest Protocol: The host country's officials may be

positioned strategically to facilitate interaction and discussions.

Elevator Etiquette

Priority for High-Ranking Officials: In elevators, high-ranking officials may be given priority for entry and exit. Ensure that they are positioned appropriately based on protocol.

Car Seating Arrangement

Official Vehicles: The head of the delegation is often seated in the rear right seat of an official vehicle, with other members arranged based on their rank.

Escort Vehicles: Security and protocol officers may accompany the delegation in separate escort vehicles.

Train Seating Arrangement

Private Compartments: High-ranking officials may be provided with private compartments for discussions and privacy during train travel. Reserved Seating: Ensure that seating arrangements in common areas are based on diplomatic protocols and hierarchy.

Protocol Officers

Escort by Protocol Officers: Delegations are often escorted by protocol officers who guide them through various events, ensuring that protocol is followed at all times.

Clear Communication: Protocol officers communicate important details, including seating arrangements, forms of address, and any specific customs or cultural considerations.

Arrival and Departure Ceremonies

Red Carpet and Honors: High-ranking officials are often received with a red carpet and honors upon arrival. The level of ceremony may vary based on the official's rank and the formality of the occasion.

Five Rules of International Protocols (5R's)

Embarking on a journey through the intricacies of international protocols, the foundation of the 5Rs—Respect, Reciprocity, Reflecting Culture, Rank, and Right—serves as a compass guiding interactions and relationships on the global stage. These principles form a tapestry of diplomatic wisdom, providing a nuanced framework for navigating the diverse landscape of international affairs. As we explore each of these pillars, we uncover the essence of diplomatic finesse, recognizing the profound impact these principles have in fostering understanding, cooperation, and mutual respect among nations and their representatives. The 5Rs encapsulate not merely a set of guidelines but a philosophy that transcends borders, shaping the dynamics of international relations with grace and wisdom.

Respect

Demonstrating respect involves recognizing and valuing the cultural diversity, customs, and traditions of participants. In the event setting, this could include considerations for cultural aspects in design, catering, and communication materials. Respecting individual preferences and creating an inclusive atmosphere contribute to the overall success of the event.

· Dietary Preferences
· Religious Practices
· Cultural Sensitivities

Reciprocity

Reciprocity emphasizes mutual respect and cooperation. In an international event, this could involve fostering partnerships and collaborations between different entities or countries. It may also extend to acknowledging and reciprocating gestures, such as hosting events in rotation among participating nations. The principle of reciprocity builds a sense of shared responsibility and mutual benefit.

· Collaborations between Participating Nations

Reflecting Culture

Reflecting culture involves incorporating elements that showcase and celebrate the diverse cultures of the participants. This might include cultural performances, exhibits, or themed decorations that highlight the rich tapestry of backgrounds represented. Ensuring cultural sensitivity in event planning contributes to a positive and inclusive experience.

· Cultural Performances
· Exhibitions

Rank

Recognizing rank in international protocol is about acknowledging the status, roles, and contributions of individuals or delegations. In the context of an event, proper protocol should be observed during formalities and ceremonies. This might include the order of speakers, seating arrangements, and introductions that reflect the hierarchical structure or official positions of participants.

· The Order of Speaker
· Seating Arrangements

Right

This principle involves giving honor to guests by placing them on the right side, a gesture that symbolizes respect and importance. In the event context, seating arrangements during formal functions or ceremonies should consider the cultural and protocol significance of placing guests of honor on the right side of the host. This can extend to VIPs, dignitaries, or individuals with special roles.

· The Right Hand Position

Understanding Cultural Differences

Understanding cultural differences in the Meetings, Incentives, Conferences, and Exhibitions (MICE) industry is paramount for the success and effectiveness of events. As MICE events attract participants from around the world, they inherently create a diverse and multicultural environment. This diversity necessitates a deep understanding of cultural differences to facilitate effective communication and collaboration among attendees with varied backgrounds.

Moreover, cultural awareness is crucial for promoting effective communication within the MICE industry. Recognizing how different cultures express ideas, convey meaning, and interpret non-verbal cues allows MICE professionals to foster clearer communication channels. This understanding reduces the risk of misunderstandings and ensures that information is conveyed accurately and appropriately.

Relationship building is a cornerstone of the MICE industry, and cultural awareness plays a pivotal role in this aspect. By recognizing and respecting cultural nuances, MICE professionals can create a positive and inclusive atmosphere, leading to stronger connections among participants, clients, and stakeholders. This cultural sensitivity helps in avoiding unintentional offense or misunderstanding of cultural norms, ensuring that events are conducted with respect for diverse practices.

The importance of cultural understanding extends to the effective design and planning of MICE events. Different cultures have varying preferences for event formats, schedules, and interactive elements. Adapting event design to accommodate these preferences enhances the overall experience for participants, making events more engaging and successful.

In the context of negotiation and business transactions, cultural awareness is indispensable. MICE events often involve participants from cultures with distinct negotiation styles, business etiquette, and decision-making processes. Understanding these differences allows professionals to navigate negotiations smoothly, fostering positive business outcomes.

Moreover, cultural awareness contributes to ensuring inclusivity in MICE events. Recognizing and accommodating diverse needs, preferences, and sensitivities creates an environment where all participants feel welcome and valued. This inclusivity is not just a matter of cultural sensitivity; it is a strategic imperative that influences the success, effectiveness, and overall impact of MICE events on a global scale.

Cultural understanding is foundational to the MICE industry, influencing communication, relationship building, event design, negotiation, and overall success. It is a key element in creating events that resonate positively with participants, clients, and stakeholders from diverse cultural backgrounds.

Review Quiz

1. Understanding Protocols in MICE Industry

What is the primary purpose of protocols in the MICE industry?

   a. To entertain participants

   b. To establish guidelines for professional conduct

   c. To create chaos during events

   d. To dictate fashion choices

2. Key Differences between Protocol and Etiquette

How does etiquette differ from protocol?

   a. Etiquette is more formal than protocol

   b. Protocol is culturally neutral, while etiquette is culture-specific

   c. Etiquette is a subset of protocol

   d. There is no difference between etiquette and protocol

3. Event-Specific Protocols

What do event-specific protocols in the MICE industry include?

   a. Only seating arrangements

   b. Guidelines for handling VIPs only

   c. Strategies for incorporating sustainable practices

   d. Strict rules against any form of technology usage

4. Five Rules of International Protocols (5R's)

What does the term "Right" in the 5Rs of international protocol refer to?

a. Human rights

b. The right side of the host

c. The right way to greet

d. The right to speak first

5. Courtesies and Hierarchical Arrangements

Where the head of the delegation is typically seated?

a. Rear left seat

b. Rear right seat

c. Front left seat

d. Front right seat

6. Understanding Cultural Differences

Why is understanding cultural differences crucial in the MICE industry?

a. It adds complexity to events.

b. It enhances the success and effectiveness of events.

c. It creates a uniform event experience.

d. It discourages diversity.

Discussion Topic

Designing Event-Specific Protocols for VIP and Dignitary Treatment

Guidelines for Group Activity

Each subgroup presents their plan for VIP and dignitary treatment.

① Introduction to VIP and Dignitary Treatment:

Begin with an overview of the significance of VIP and dignitary treatment in event management.

Discuss how positive experiences for high-profile guests contribute to the overall success of an event.

② Identification of VIP and Dignitary Areas:

Brainstorm and identify specific areas within an event that are crucial for VIP and dignitary treatment.

Examples: Accommodations, transportation, designated event spaces, and personalized services.

③ Analyzing Cultural Sensitivity:

Discuss the importance of cultural sensitivity when designing protocols for VIPs and dignitaries. Consider how cultural differences may influence expectations and preferences in treatment.

④ Prioritization and Customization:

Prioritize areas that require specific attention and customization for VIPs and dignitaries. Discuss how protocols may differ based on the nature of the event and the preferences of the guests.

⑤ Security and Privacy Considerations:

Discuss security measures and privacy considerations for high-profile guests. Consider the balance between providing personalized services and ensuring the safety and privacy of VIPs.

⑥ Designing Exclusive Experiences:

Brainstorm ways to design exclusive experiences for VIPs and dignitaries during the event.

5. STRATEGIC MICE MANAGEMENT WITH TEMPLATES

Advantages of Templates in MICE Management

Templates play a pivotal role in the realm of MICE (Meetings, Incentives, Conferences, and Exhibitions) management, offering a myriad of advantages that contribute to the efficiency, consistency, and professionalism of the event planning process. At the core of their significance is the element of consistency, where templates provide a standardized format across various documents and communications. This uniformity ensures a cohesive and professional appearance throughout the event, creating a lasting and positive brand image.

Beyond aesthetics, the time efficiency gained through templates is a notable advantage. By providing pre-designed structures, templates eliminate the need to create documents from scratch for each event, allowing event organizers to focus their efforts on more intricate and event-specific details. This time-saving aspect significantly streamlines the planning process, enabling a more efficient use of resources.

The professional presentation facilitated by templates contributes to the overall credibility of event-related documents and materials. Whether it's an invitation, an agenda, or presentation slides, a well-designed template enhances the professionalism of these elements. Additionally, templates can be tailored to align with the event's brand identity, incorporating specific colors, logos, and fonts. This consistent branding reinforces the event's identity, leaving a lasting impression on participants and stakeholders.

Templates also play a crucial role in communication, providing a structured framework for conveying information. Clear and concise communication is vital in event management, and templates help achieve this by presenting important details in an organized manner. This not only reduces the likelihood of misunderstandings but also enhances collaboration among stakeholders, sponsors, participants, and team members.

Adaptability is another key feature of templates, allowing them to be customized for various stages of event planning. Whether it's pre-event invitations, during-event presentations, or post-event surveys, templates offer flexibility to meet specific needs. In the context of risk reduction, templates help minimize errors or oversights in critical documents by providing predefined structures that ensure essential information is consistently included.

Finally, templates contribute to post-event analysis by offering a structured approach to gathering feedback and analyzing outcomes. Templates for surveys and reports streamline the post-event evaluation process, enabling organizers to compare results across different events for continuous improvement. In essence, the strategic use of templates in MICE management serves as a valuable tool for maintaining standards, saving time, and presenting a cohesive and well-organized event experience.

☐ Overview

Advantages of Templates in MICE Management

- · Consistency
- · Time Efficiency
- · Professionalism
- · Brand Identity
- · Communication
- · Adaptability
- · Risk Reduction
- · Post-Event Analysis

Pre-Event

【Example】 Invitation Letter

Subject: Invitation to Keynote Speech at MICE Industry Conference

Dear Professor [Full Name],

I trust this message finds you well. I am [Your Name], the conference planner for the MICE Industry Development Conference, scheduled from March 1 to March 8, 2024, at the COEX Convention & Exhibition Center in Seoul, Korea.

We are impressed by your expertise in [Speaker's field of expertise] and would be honored to have you deliver a keynote speech, sharing insights on the MICE industry's current landscape and future trends.

Event Details:
Date: March 1 to March 8, 2024
Venue: COEX Convention & Exhibition Center, Seoul, Korea
Your participation would greatly enhance our conference, and we are committed to accommodating any requirements you may have. If you can accept our invitation, kindly inform us of your availability and any preferences.

We look forward to the possibility of your presence, making our conference a memorable and enriching experience.

Best regards,
[Your Full Name]
[Your Title/Organization/Contact Information]

【Example】 RSVP (Response) Form

Subject: RSVP Request: Iftar Dinner Event on April 2, 2025

Dear [Guest's Name],

We hope this message finds you well. You are cordially invited to our Iftar dinner event in celebration of Ramadan week on April 2, 2025, at the Marriott Hotel.

Kindly confirm your attendance by March 15, and let us know of any dietary preferences or restrictions:

☐ Attending with no dietary restrictions.
☐ Attending with dietary preferences or restrictions: [Specify].
☐ Regrettably, unable to attend.

Your timely response is appreciated, and we look forward to hosting you at this special event.

Best regards,

[Your Full Name]
[Your Title]
Korean Ministry of Foreign Affairs
[Contact Information]

【Example】 Official Letter to Participants

Subject: Invitation to Korea's Advanced Electronic Information Technology Exhibition

Dear [Recipient's Name],

We are thrilled to invite you to the exhibition displaying Korea's cutting-edge electronic information technology at KINTEX from August 5 to August 10, 2024.

Conference Features:
Korean ICT experts and startup CEOs as speakers
Exclusive Offer:
The first pre-registered attendee receives a Starbucks gift card worth 20,000 won. To secure your spot and a chance to receive the gift card, please register on our website.

We look forward to your participation in this exciting showcase of technological innovation.

Best regards,

[Your Full Name]
[Your Title]
[Event/Organization Name]
[Contact Information]

During-Event

【Example】 Session Evaluation Form

Event: [Event Name]
Date: [Date]
Session Title: [Session Title]
Speaker/Facilitator: [Speaker/Facilitator Name]

Instructions:
Please take a moment to provide your feedback on the session you attended. Your input is valuable and will help us enhance the quality of future events. Thank you!

1. Session Relevance:
How relevant was the content to your professional interests or needs?
☐ Not at all relevant
☐ Somewhat relevant
☐ Very relevant
☐ Extremely relevant

2. Content Clarity:
How clear and understandable was the presentation/content?
☐ Not clear at all
☐ Somewhat clear
☐ Very clear
☐ Extremely clear

3. Speaker/Facilitator:
Rate the speaker/facilitator on their knowledge and delivery:
☐ Poor

- [ ] Fair
- [ ] Good
- [ ] Excellent

4. Session Engagement:

How engaging was the session in terms of interactive elements (Q&A, discussions, etc.)?
- [ ] Not engaging at all
- [ ] Somewhat engaging
- [ ] Very engaging
- [ ] Extremely engaging

5. Session Length:

Was the session too short, too long, or just right?
- [ ] Too short
- [ ] Too long
- [ ] Just right

6. Key Takeaways:

What were the key takeaways for you from this session?
[Open Text Response]

7. Suggestions for Improvement:

Any suggestions for improving the session content or delivery?
[Open Text Response]

Thank you for taking the time to complete this evaluation. Your feedback is invaluable to us. If you have additional comments or would like to provide further feedback, please feel free to contact us directly.

【Example】 **Speaker Agreement**

Event Organizer:

[Your Organization Name]

[Your Address/City, State, Zip Code]

[Email Address/Phone Number]

Speaker:

[Speaker's Full Name]

[Speaker's Address/City, State, Zip Code]

[Email Address/Phone Number]

Event Details:

[Event Name/Dates/Venue]

1. Services:

The Speaker agrees to provide services as a speaker at the above-stated event. This includes delivering a presentation on the agreed-upon topic.

2. Compensation:

In consideration of the services provided, the Event Organizer agrees to compensate the Speaker as follows:

[Specify compensation details, e.g., honorarium, travel expenses, accommodation, etc.]

3. Presentation Materials:

The Speaker agrees to provide any necessary presentation materials by [Agreed Date], including slides, handouts, or other materials required for the presentation.

4. Promotion:

The Speaker grants the Event Organizer the right to use their name, image, and biography for promotional purposes related to the event.

5. Travel and Accommodation:

If applicable, the Event Organizer agrees to cover reasonable travel expenses and accommodation for the Speaker in accordance with the terms outlined in [Section 2].

6. Cancellation:

In the event that either party needs to cancel this agreement, written notice must be provided at least [Number of Days] days prior to the event.

7. Confidentiality:

Both parties agree to keep confidential any proprietary or sensitive information disclosed during the preparation or delivery of the presentation.

8. Governing Law:

This Agreement shall be governed by and construed in accordance with the laws of [State/Country].

9. Entire Agreement:

This Agreement constitutes the entire understanding between the parties and supersedes all prior agreements, whether written or oral.

10. Signatures:

The parties have executed this Speaker Agreement as of the date first above written.

[Speaker's Signature]

【Example】 **Sponsorship Proposal**

[Your Organization's Logo]

Sponsorship Proposal

[Event Name/Program Title]

[Event Date(s) or Program Duration] | [Location/Venue]

About [Your Organization]

[Provide a brief overview of your organization, its mission, and its impact.]

Event/Program Overview

[Describe the event or program, its purpose, target audience, and expected attendance. Highlight the unique aspects that make it an attractive sponsorship opportunity.]

Sponsorship Levels

1. Platinum Sponsor - [Amount]

Logo placement on all event-marketing materials.

Exclusive sponsor of [specific event feature or session].

Social media mentions and recognition during the opening/closing ceremony.

2. Gold Sponsor - [Amount]

Logo placement on event collateral and website.

Sponsorship of a specific program element or session.

Social media mentions and recognition in event-related press releases.

3. Silver Sponsor - [Amount]

Logo placement on event materials.

Sponsorship of a specific event segment or area.

Social media mentions and recognition on the event website.

4. Bronze Sponsor - [Amount]

Logo placement on select event materials.

Recognition during the event.

Social media mentions.

Benefits for Sponsors

Brand Exposure: Reach a diverse audience through our marketing channels.

Networking Opportunities: Engage with industry leaders and professionals.

Media Recognition: Receive coverage in event-related press releases and media outreach.

Our Commitment to Sponsors

[Explain how your organization will ensure sponsors receive the agreed-upon benefits, including timelines for logo placement, social media mentions, and other promotional activities.]

Next Steps

[Include contact information for inquiries and express your interest in discussing customized sponsorship packages to meet the potential sponsor's specific needs.]

Thank you for considering [Your Organization] as your partner. We look forward to the opportunity to work together and create a mutually beneficial partnership.

Feel free to add visuals, graphs, or any other relevant information that would enhance your proposal. Make sure to tailor the proposal to the specific details and offerings of your event or program.

【Example】 Exhibition Booth Reservation Form

[Event Name/Exhibition Title]

Exhibition Date: [Event Dates]

Venue: [Event Venue]

Exhibitor Information:

Company/Organization Name:

Contact Person:

Contact Email:

Contact Phone:

Address:

Website:

Booth Reservation Details:

Preferred Booth Size:

☐ Standard Booth (10'x10')

☐ Double Booth (20'x10')

☐ Custom Size (Specify: _____)

Booth Location Preference:

☐ Corner Booth (if available)

☐ Near Entrance

☐ Near [Specific Feature/Area]

☐ No Preference

Booth Equipment/Additional Requirements:

☐ Table and Chairs

☐ Electrical Outlets

☐ Wi-Fi Access

☐ Other (Specify: _____)

Additional Options:

Sponsorship Opportunities:

☐ Title Sponsor

☐ Session Sponsor
☐ Lanyard Sponsor
☐ Other (Specify: _____)

Advertising Opportunities:
☐ Event Program Ad
☐ Website Banner Ad
☐ Social Media Promotion
☐ Other (Specify: _____)

Payment Details:
Total Booth Cost: [Amount]
Payment Method:
☐ Credit Card
☐ Bank Transfer
☐ Other (Specify: _____)

Terms and Conditions:
· Booth reservations are confirmed upon receipt of payment.
· Booth assignments will be made based on availability and preferences.
· Cancellation policy: [Specify your cancellation policy,
  e.g., Refundable until [Date]].
· Exhibitors are responsible for any damages to the booth space or
  equipment.

By submitting this form, the exhibitor agrees to abide by the terms and
conditions outlined above.

Signature:
[Digital Signature or Space for Manual Signature]

Date:
[Date]

Post-Event

【Example】 Event Survey

[Event Name/Title]

Thank you for attending [Event Name]! Your feedback is important to us, and we appreciate you taking the time to share your thoughts. Please complete the following survey to help us improve future events.

1. Event Satisfaction

Overall, how satisfied were you with [Event Name]?

☐ Very Satisfied

☐ Satisfied

☐ Neutral

☐ Dissatisfied

☐ Very Dissatisfied

2. Event Content

How would you rate the relevance and quality of the event content?

☐ Excellent

☐ Good

☐ Average

☐ Poor

3. Speakers/Presenters

Rate the effectiveness of the speakers/presenters.

☐ Excellent

☐ Good

☐ Average

☐ Poor

4. Organization and Logistics

How well organized was the event in terms of logistics (registration, scheduling, etc.)?

☐ Very Well-Organized

- [ ] Well-Organized
- [ ] Somewhat Organized
- [ ] Poorly Organized

5. Venue

Rate the venue facilities and amenities

- [ ] Excellent
- [ ] Good
- [ ] Average
- [ ] Poor

6. Networking Opportunities

How would you rate the networking opportunities provided at the event?

- [ ] Excellent
- [ ] Good
- [ ] Average
- [ ] Poor

7. Suggestions for Improvement

What aspects of the event could be improved, and how?

[Open Text Response]

8. Likelihood of Recommending:

How likely are you to recommend [Event Name] to a colleague or friend?

- [ ] Very Likely
- [ ] Likely
- [ ] Neutral
- [ ] Unlikely
- [ ] Very Unlikely

9. Additional Comments:

Do you have any additional comments or suggestions for future events?

[Open Text Response]

Demographic Information (Optional):

10. Your Role/Position

☐ Attendee

☐ Speaker

☐ Exhibitor

☐ Other (Specify: _____)

11. How did you hear about the event?

☐ Email

☐ Social Media

☐ Word of Mouth

☐ Other (Specify: _____)

Thank you for your valuable feedback! Your input helps us enhance future events.

【Example】Thank You Letter
[Your Organization's Name]
[Your Organization's Address/City, State, Zip Code]
[Date]
[Participant/Sponsor/Partner Name]
[Participant/Sponsor/Partner Organization]
[Address/City, State, Zip Code]

Dear [Participant/Sponsor/Partner Name],

Subject: Thank You for Your Contribution to [Event Name]

I extend heartfelt thanks for your pivotal role in making [Event Name] a success. Your [attendance/sponsorship/partnership] significantly enriched the event, and we are grateful for the [positive atmosphere/networking opportunities/educational content] you brought.

Your [dedication/support/engagement] made a lasting impact, and we appreciate the [specific details or highlights] you contributed. We look forward to the possibility of future collaborations.

Thank you for being a crucial part of [Event Name]. Your [dedication/support/partnership] is truly appreciated.

Warm regards,

[Your Full Name]
[Your Title/Your Organization]
[Contact Information]

【Example】 Post-Event Press Release

FOR IMMEDIATE RELEASE
[Date]
Contact:
[Your Full Name]
[Your Title/Your Organization]
[Contact Information]

[Event Name] Celebrates Success with Unforgettable Highlights

[City, State] — [Date] — [Your Organization] is thrilled to announce the successful conclusion of [Event Name], held on [Event Date] at [Event Venue]. The event brought together [number of participants] participants and [number of sponsors] sponsors, making it a [highlight or theme] extravaganza.

Key Highlights:

· Record Attendance:
[Event Name] attracted [number of attendees], setting a new record for participant engagement.

· Inspirational Speakers:
Renowned speakers, including [Speaker 1], [Speaker 2], and [Speaker 3], captivated the audience with insightful talks on [topics].

· Cutting-Edge Exhibitions:
The exhibition area showcased the latest innovations in [industry/topic], featuring [number of exhibitors] exhibitors and drawing interest from [number of visitors] visitors.

· Networking Success:
Participants enjoyed ample networking opportunities, fostering valuable connections within the [industry/community].

· Sponsor Appreciation:

We extend our heartfelt gratitude to our [Gold/Silver/Bronze] sponsors, [List of Sponsors], whose support was integral to the success of [Event Name].

· Community Impact:

[Event Name] also made a positive impact on the community by [highlight any community-related activities or initiatives].

Quotes:

[Include a quote from an organizer, speaker, or participant expressing gratitude or highlighting the event's impact.]

About [Your Organization]:

[Include a brief paragraph about your organization, its mission, and any relevant background.]

Next Steps:

[Include information about future events or initiatives, and encourage media contacts to reach out for additional information.]

Press Contact:

[Your Full Name]

[Your Title/Your Organization]

[Contact Information]

Review Quiz

Advantages of Templates in MICE Management

1. Why is consistency important in MICE management documents?

a. It adds complexity.

b. It establishes a professional image and brand identity.

c. It discourages creativity.

d. It makes documents too uniform.

2. What is a key benefit of using templates in terms of time efficiency?

a. Templates create more work.

b. Templates slow down the planning process.

c. Templates eliminate the need to create documents from scratch.

d. Templates only work for specific events.

3. How do templates contribute to professionalism in event-related materials?

a. They introduce errors.

b. They discourage a polished presentation.

c. They hinder communication.

d. They enhance the credibility of materials.

4. In the context of templates, what does "adaptability" refer to?

a. Templates are rigid and inflexible.

b. Templates can only be used for pre-event materials.

c. Templates can be customized for various stages of event planning.

d. Templates are limited to specific industries.

5. Why is risk reduction listed as an advantage of using templates?

a. Templates increase errors.

b. Templates create inconsistencies.

c. Templates help minimize errors in critical documents.

d. Templates are irrelevant to risk reduction.

6. What is the role of templates in post-event analysis?

a. Templates hinder feedback collection.

b. Templates are only useful for pre-event documents.

c. Templates streamline feedback collection and outcome analysis.

d. Templates are unnecessary for continuous improvement.

Discussion Topic

Writing an Invitation Letter for a University Festival Guest Speaker

Objective:

The objective of this group discussion is to collaboratively draft an effective invitation letter for a guest speaker to be invited to our university festival. The letter should be compelling, informative, and professionally written to ensure a positive response from the potential speaker.

Guidelines:

☐ Introduction

Begin with a brief introduction to the purpose of the discussion.

Discuss the significance of having a guest speaker at the university festival. Emphasize the importance of a well-crafted invitation letter.

☐ Understanding the Audience

Identify the target audience for the festival and the likely interests of the attendees. Discuss the type of speaker who would resonate well with the university community.

Consider any specific themes or topics that align with the festival's goals.

☐ Key Information

List the essential details to be included in the invitation letter:

· Event details: Date, time, and venue of the university festival.
· Introduction to the festival: Highlight its purpose and significance.
· Speaker's role: Clarify the expectations and role of the guest speaker.
· Benefits: Mention the benefits for the speaker in participating in the festival.

☐ Crafting the Invitation

Brainstorm ideas for a compelling and engaging introduction to the invitation letter. Collaboratively draft the body of the letter, ensuring clarity and professionalism.

Include persuasive language that highlights the uniqueness of the university festival. Emphasize how the speaker's expertise aligns with the festival's theme or goals.

☐ Polishing and Review

Review the drafted letter for clarity, grammar, and coherence.

Ensure that the tone is respectful, inviting, and aligns with the university's values. Discuss any additional elements that could enhance the invitation.

NOTE AND SUGGESTIONS

Congratulations on reaching the end of this book. I hope this journey through the MICE industry has provided valuable insights and knowledge about the diverse and dynamic world of event management. As you embark on or continue your exploration of the MICE industry, consider the following notes and suggestions.

STAY INFORMED
The MICE industry is ever evolving, with new trends, technologies, and best practices emerging regularly. Stay informed by following industry publications, attending conferences, and engaging with relevant online forums.

NETWORKING IS KEY
Building a strong professional network is crucial in the MICE industry. Attend industry events, join professional organizations, and connect with peers and mentors. Networking opens doors to opportunities and enriches your understanding of the field.

CONTINUED EDUCATION
Consider pursuing additional education and certifications in event management or related fields. Many institutions offer

specialized courses that can enhance your skills and make you more competitive in the job market.

GAIN PRATICAL EXPERIENCE

Practical experience is invaluable in the MICE industry. Seek internships, volunteer for events, or work on small projects to apply your knowledge and build a portfolio. Practical experience will set you apart when entering the job market.

READ INDUSTRY LITERATURE

Explore books, articles, and case studies related to event management, leadership, and industry trends.

Remember, the MICE industry is a dynamic and exciting field that thrives on creativity, organization, and adaptability. Whether you're a student or a seasoned professional, continuous learning and a passion for creating memorable experiences will propel you toward success.

Wishing you a fulfilling and prosperous journey in the MICE industry ☺

REVIEW QUIZ ANSWERS KEY

1. UNDERSTANDING MICE INDUSTRY

b. Latin word conventio

c. Conventions only involve conferences,
   while MICE includes various components.

c. To enhance professionalism, quality, and global recognition.

c. By attracting visitors, generating economic activity,
   and fostering growth.

a. Incentives

b. The interconnected outcomes stemming from hosting
   impactful business events.

2. KEY STAKEHOLDERS OF THE MICE INDUSTRY

b. Event planning and execution

b. Promoting and marketing a destination

a. Narrow specialization

c. Gaining visibility and promoting brands

c. Versatility in hosting different types of events

c. Promoting and managing a destination

3. MICE MASTERY: SIX STEPS TO EVENT SUCCESS

c. Gathering insights for decision-making

d. Identifying event objectives and activities

c. To ensure seamless execution

c. Marketing and advertising

c. Overseeing event logistics

a. Setting benchmarks for success

4. PROTOCOL IN MICE INDUSTRY

b. To establish guidelines for professional conduct

c. Etiquette is a subset of protocol

c. Strategies for incorporating sustainable practices

b. The right side of the host

b. Rear right seat

b. It enhances the success and effectiveness of events.

5. STRATEGIC MICE MANAGEMENT WITH TEMPLATES

b. It establishes a professional image and brand identity.

c. Templates eliminate the need to create documents from scratch.

d. They enhance the credibility of materials.

c. Templates can be customized for various stages of event planning.

c. Templates help minimize errors in critical documents.

c. Templates streamline feedback collection and outcome analysis.

REFERENCES

· Ahmed, S. (2020). The Exploration of New Avenues Toward Better Business Management: A Business Tourism Perspective. In Accelerating Knowledge Sharing, Creativity, and Innovation Through Business Tourism (pp. 281-297). IGI Global.

· Dev, N. K., Shankar, R., Zacharia, Z. G., & Swami, S. (2021). Supply chain resilience for managing the ripple effect in Industry 4.0 for green product diffusion. International Journal of Physical Distribution & Logistics Management, 51(8), 897-930.

· Düffelmeyer, F., Hildebrandt, M. (2011). M.I.C.E.. In: Papathanassis, A. (eds) The Long Tail of Tourism. Gabler. https://doi.org/10.1007/978-3-8349-6231-7_14.

· Dolgui, A., & Ivanov, D. (2021). Ripple effect and supply chain disruption management: new trends and research directions. International Journal of Production Research, 59(1), 102-109.

· Foltz, C. J., & Ullman-Cullere, M. (1999). Guidelines for assessing the health and condition of mice. Lab animal, 28(5).

· Fox, S., & Comeau-Vallée, M. (2020). The negotiation of sharing leadership in the context of professional hierarchy: Interactions on interprofessional teams. Leadership, 16(5), 568-591.

· Gregoric, M. (2014). PESTEL analysis of tourism destinations in the perspective of business tourism (MICE). In Faculty of Tourism and Hospitality Management in Opatija. Biennial International Congress. Tourism & Hospitality Industry (p. 551). University of Rijeka, Faculty of Tourism & Hospitality Management.

· Jain, S. (2022). Feedback and Debriefing. In: Biyani, C.S., Van Cleynenbreugel, B., Mottrie, A. (eds) Practical Simulation in Urology . Springer, Cham. https://doi.org/10.1007/978-3-030-88789-6_22

· Jugănaru, I. D. (2022). Recent Evolutions and Trends in the Trade

Fairs and Exhibitions Industry, before and after the COVID-19 Pandemic. The ROMEXPO Company's Case (Romania). Economics, 6.

· Kim, K., & Ko, D. (2020). How to build a sustainable MICE environment based on social identity theory. Sustainability, 12(17), 7166.

· Kim, E. G., Chhabra, D., & Timothy, D. J. (2022). Towards a Creative MICE Tourism Destination Branding Model: Integrating Heritage Tourism in New Orleans, USA. Sustainability, 14(24), 16411.

· Kitchen, E. (2022). Strategic event planning. In The Routledge Handbook of Business Events (pp. 32-42). Routledge.

· Koob, C. (2021). Determinants of content marketing effectiveness: Conceptual framework and empirical findings from a managerial perspective. PloS one, 16(4), e0249457.

· Ladkin, A. (2006). Conference tourism-MICE market and business tourism. In Tourism business frontiers (pp. 56-66). Routledge.

Mair, J. (2015). Incentive travel: A theoretical perspective. Event Management, 19(4), 543-552.

· Liu, X., Seevers, R., & Lin, H. (2022). Employability skills for MICE management in the context of ICTs. Plos one, 17(7), e0271430.

· Locke, M. (2012). Strategic Planning and Management for the MICE Sector: A Case Study of the Auckland Region (Doctoral dissertation, University of Waikato).

· Market, V. F. (2016). Global Opportunity Analysis and Industry Forecast, 2017-2023. Allied Market Research: Pune, India.

· Nolan, E. (2020). The supply and design of different types of venues for business events. International Journal of Tourism Cities, 6(4), 691-710.

· OpenStax. (2018). Introduction to Business by OpenStax (paperback version, B&W) First Edition. OpenStax.

· Sable, K., Roy, A., & Deshmukh, R. (2019). MICE industry by event type (Meetings, Incentives, Conventions, and Exhibitions): global opportunity analysis and industry forecast, 2018-2025. Allied Mark Res, 1-136.

· Schoemann, M., Lüken, M., Grage, T., Kieslich, P. J., & Scherbaum, S. (2019). Validating mouse-tracking: How design factors influence action dynamics in intertemporal decision making. Behavior Research Methods, 51, 2356-2377.

· Smith, J. (2019). Communication at Work: A College-to-Career Guide to Success. Ecampus Ontario, 2019.

· Stopford, B. (2018). Designing event-driven systems. O'Reilly Media, Incorporated.

· Swanson, M. M., Wohl, A., Pope, L., Grance, T., Hash, J., & Thomas, R. (2002). Contingency planning guide for information technology systems.

· Te Yi Chang , I Ying Tsai (2020). Language Management in MICE Industries. Universal Journal of Management, 8(4), 146 - 159.

· Trišić, I., & Arsenov-Bojović, V. (2018, June). The role of MICE industry in tourism development. In Tourism International Scientific Conference Vrnjačka Banja-TISC (Vol. 3, No. 2, pp. 275-293).

· UKEssays. (November 2018). Meetings Incentives Conferences And Exhibitions In The Uk Tourism Essay. Retrieved from https://www.ukessays.com/essays/tourism/meetings-incentives-conferences-and-exhibitions-in-the-uk-tourism-essay.php?vref=1

· Urvashi Atri (2021). MICE Marketing & Management. Quest Journals, 9(7), 69-76.

· Wang, M., & Luo, Q. (2018). Exploring the MICE industry career path. International Journal of Contemporary Hospitality Management, 30(5), 2308-2326.

https://www.etymonline.com/

https://en.wiktionary.org/wiki/convention

https://hospitalityinsights.ehl.edu/

https://www.micecapabilities.com/micestandards/

https://koreaconvention.org:8090/eng/engmain.kc

https://www.skillsyouneed.com/ips/meetings.html

https://www.worldpco.org/index.php?option=com_content&view=article&id=86&Itemid=294

https://www.gevme.com/en/blog/trade-show-exhibition-planning-guide/

https://streetfightmag.com/2022/03/17/the-evolution-of-sponsorships-in-the-event-industry/

https://stova.io/event-sponsorship-guide/

https://www.britannica.com/topic/regulatory-agency

https://www.lawinsider.com/dictionary/governmental-regulatory-body

https://www.gov.uk/government/publications/international-regulatory-cooperation-strategy/international-regulatory-cooperation-strategy

https://www.oecd.org/gov/regulatory-policy/international-regulatory-co-operation-5b28b589-en.htm

https://www.solimarinternational.com/what-is-a-destination-management-organization-dmo-and-why-should-destinations-care/

https://www.unwto.org/policy-destination-management

https://www.tourismtiger.com/blog/what-are-convention-and-visitors-bureaus-and-how-can-they-help-your-business/

https://www.gacvb.com/what-is-a-cvb-

https://www.eventbrite.com/blog/event-design-important-skill-ds00/

https://www.forbes.com/sites/forbesbusinesscouncil/2022/12/06/seven-tips-for-building-a-themed-interactive-event-experience/?sh=76d812ba23ab

https://taxivaxi.com/guides/mastering-mice-a-success-guide-to-planning-events/

https://www.citynationplace.com/five-steps-for-any-destination-looking-to-attract-mice-travel-in-2022

https://www.mlit.go.jp/kankocho/en/shisaku/kokusai/mice.html

https://asana.com/ko/resources/promotion-strategy

https://research.g2.com/insights/event-management-trends-2024

https://crm.org/news/best-event-management-software